IDENTITY REDEMPTION

D<small>ANIELLE</small> D<small>E</small>G<small>ARMO</small>

ISBN 979-8-89243-842-1 (paperback)
ISBN 979-8-89243-843-8 (digital)

Copyright © 2024 by Danielle DeGarmo

All rights reserved. No part of this publication may be reproduced, distributed, or transmitted in any form or by any means, including photocopying, recording, or other electronic or mechanical methods without the prior written permission of the publisher. For permission requests, solicit the publisher via the address below.

Christian Faith Publishing
832 Park Avenue
Meadville, PA 16335
www.christianfaithpublishing.com

Printed in the United States of America

This book is dedicated partly to Anthony Hust, who promised/threatened to follow me around with a SpongeBob meme shirt that said "Boo!" if this book wasn't out. Now, he can spend his money on this book instead of a shirt! Thanks for being part of the pull to write, brother. You told me that thinkers are important in this world, and the only people more important are doers. Then you told me I was both. Thank you for speaking life into this book and into me. God used you in this story. (Insert handshake emoji and salute.)

INTRODUCTION

This book has been written and rewritten, words rearranged, chapters scrapped, and completely transformed more times than I found to be even slightly convenient or would like to admit. The book in your hands, on your screen, or that you're listening to is not the book I set out to write when I began. I began writing this book as another box to check on my to-do list to be successful. I began writing this book to place "author" under my list of titles I once found identity in. I began writing this book as if I was the main character. I began writing this book because if it sells, that's passive income, and who wouldn't want that? But this book is not for me. This book isn't even really about me. If it was, I don't think it wouldn't be in your hands right now. So maybe it's for you.

I am writing this book simply because God said to, though my brother in Christ, Anthony, did tell me he'd follow me around in a SpongeBob meme shirt that said "Boo!" if I didn't, and honestly, it's something he would do. But, no, really, I am writing this book simply because God said to. He put it on my heart, and originally, I took it and ran with the wrong intentions. I spent almost a year chasing the wind, trying to write a book. When I was convicted by my reason for writing though, I rejected the idea and scrapped the book altogether. I couldn't find the words. And every time I thought I had figured it out, I was just left more frustrated. I wasn't writing simply because God said to; I was writing because God said to, and x, y, and z were in it for me. I said, "Good idea, God!" and attempted to take over. Have you ever done something like that?

I remember in elementary school, in art class or during a project, when the teacher would lay out all the supplies but hadn't given instructions yet. Many of us would get super excited and start grabbing the supplies before knowing what to do with them, and that's what I did, at first, with this book. I took the supplies, or the idea, into my own hands before I knew what the project was, and I decided it was for x, y, and z. I tried to figure out what to write, what the project instructions were, and what the plan was without paying attention or listening. Instead of leaning into the one who already had a perfect plan, God, I tried to make my own. And when I didn't have a plan, I didn't know the point. So I prayed. And as I started writing the book, GOD TOOK OVER. The question then was, would I try to split the throne with God or surrender it?

CHAPTER 1

OUT OF ORDER

I surrendered the throne, and He told me to tell my story. I didn't know where to begin. He told me to tell my story, and I laughed and asked, "Which one?" Little did I know, it'd be the one He'd write in the midst of this seemingly small "side surrender." It is the one He has rewritten for me. By "side surrender," I mean I *said* I was letting God drive but never got out of the driver's seat. Have you ever sat in a parent's or relative's lap as a kid and got to "drive" the car, truck, or tractor? God's not that gullible. I let go of the wheel but was stomping on the brakes. I wasn't fooling Him or even myself. That's "side surrender," not surrender.

God made it clear to me on the morning of October 26, 2023, that He wanted my surrender, not just in this book but in my life. He was asking for more than a side surrender. I had the choice to get out of the driver's seat. And because I did, you're reading or listening to this book. I'm not the main character of this story nor the author. Despite what the world tells us and what it's so easy to believe and act like, we are not the main characters in our lives. Once I got out of the driver's seat, I realized I had it all out of order. My relationships, my priorities, my perspective, and my identity were all out of order.

On October 26, 2023, I quit my job with no notice to write a book, this book, that I wasn't entirely sure what it'd be about at the time. Quitting my job was not the first decision I made that day but the second. What came first is what finally gave me a clear point for the book I am writing; it's what put everything back in order. And spoiler alert: It was God.

On October 26, I woke up and lost track of time, just a bit, in my morning devotional and prayer. But no worries yet, as I would just skip the makeup and make it out the door on my way to work. Then, not giving myself enough time for "what if," I got stopped at the train tracks—my fault. But my thought in the moment was, *Of course the train would pass through this morning of all mornings!* I raced into the office, rushed, annoyed, and made it to the parking lot, late. It was 8:30 a.m., and our morning meeting began at 8:30 a.m. I was probably fine to just head inside and barely make it to the meeting on time. But as my heart began to race, my face quivered, and hands shook. I texted my manager at 8:31 that I was in the parking lot, having an anxiety attack. I told him that I would be up as soon as I could. I thought I *was* having an anxiety attack. My heart rate was well above 100bpm. My smartwatch told me, "Stress seems high! Try some breathing exercises?" Ha! Being late could have very easily brought on an anxiety attack for me. But this was not an anxiety attack. I wasn't anxious but more annoyed and overwhelmed. I realized quickly, God was trying to get my attention, and my attitude quickly changed.

I sat in my car, and I leaned into what originally felt like a disruption in my morning. I prayed, and I worshipped. I prayed, and I cried. And before I knew it, I was shaking and trembling in a moment of spiritual warfare, hearing God's voice and wrestling with fear and doubt. So I just kept crying out to God and worshipping. I welcomed the interruption, and I leaned into His voice, knowing there was a spiritual encounter to be had. When God told me to quit my job and devote my time to finishing the book I'd set out to write, I was so confident it was His voice, but I wanted to be sure.

IDENTITY REDEMPTION

Every doubt and fear you can imagine popped in. Everything that I set out to write in this book and everything that I had written already was being tested at this very moment. The side surrender was now a complete surrender.

For context, I would not be quitting a job waitressing or working retail, though not to take light away from honest jobs. This was a job with more opportunity than I had the experience for. I was an insurance agent, licensed in multiple states, with no college degree at nineteen years old. I was a professional making good money and this job provided a lot for me. I walked into the interview at eighteen years old, fresh out of high school, in a bright pink pantsuit, declaring that I had no experience. I started as a marketing assistant and moved my way up. The story of how I even came to that interview is another story of God's doing that you should ask me about sometime. But I had to ask, do I trust God as a provider *first?* Will I remain in the driver's seat, on the throne, or will I surrender?

I called a trusted woman from my home church—her name is Tara—and I asked her to pray with me. She was already crying from being wrecked by the Holy Spirit that morning as well and asked what I wanted prayer for or if I just wanted to let the Spirit lead. I told her to let the Spirit lead, and, oh, did the Holy Spirit lead. We prayed for me to say yes (a lot of yeses), for clear eyes, for ears shut to anything but the Father's voice, and for a season of "sprinting." If sprinting is another term for making fast, impulsive decisions, like quitting my job without notice, I sure was sprinting. So I quit my job, and this book is the result and the story God's given me to tell. I walked into my manager's office, two hours late, mind you, just hoping he might go ahead and fire me. I actually prayed to be fired. But I didn't get fired. He already knew. He said, "You quittin'?" I told him everything I just told you, in fewer sentences and with more awkward laughs, signed the papers, said my goodbyes, and prayed with a sweet coworker. I was officially unemployed, but that was not my identity.

To say this took a lot of faith is true and false. I was honestly in a situation with the resources to quit this job and be okay financially. I would thankfully not be struggling by any means. I didn't have any dependents, and I was single. I was so annoyed at my singleness, by the way, for so long until I realized both marriage and singleness are blessings from God. God wanted my undivided attention in this season or maybe forever, I'm not sure. But this job was an answer to many prayers, and the worries began to flood my mind. I felt like, by getting this job, I had come a long way and wondered, would I be starting all over? I would go from being above average for my age to below average. My financial status wouldn't take as big of a blow as my pride would.

Quitting my job was humbling because in it, God showed me the people and things I had put on pedestals, what I worshipped, and where I placed my identity. I claimed it was God, but my life claimed otherwise. This job wasn't a problem though. It was a blessing and an answered prayer when I got it and when I quit. The environment was unreal and above and beyond everything I had prayed for. The people in that office made such an impact on me in a tough season of my life. I prayed, "God, you gave me this job. Why would I quit? This job saved me." Oh, that's why. I was worshipping the provision, not the provider.

Have you ever done that, prayed long and hard for something, and then when you get it, you worship the answer to the prayer instead of the one who answered your prayer? This put into perspective for me the entire point of this book. This is a story of identity redemption.

So I quit my job to write this book. But really, I just said yes to God. The devotional I had been reading at this time is a book written by Lysa TerKeurst called *What Happens When Women Say Yes to God and Walk in Faith*. Little did I know, what happens when you say yes to God is that you might quit your job, ha!

I've had to remember that I got this job in the first place because of God. God has used this job to provide for me and show me His love, goodness, grace, and sweetness, but I will hold onto God, not onto this job. He is the reason I had this job and the reason I left this job, and I wouldn't have it any other way. Everything I have is God's to begin with, including my story. I am not the main character. Anything I think I've earned or accomplished—I must remember—is because God gave me the ability. My life is not my own, for I belong to the Lord.

> God owns it all. We are simply managers of His resources. (Lysa TerKeurst)

When I first became a Christian, I tried to do all the right things, but it didn't matter until I got first things first. I have to remember that the commandments only matter because of who the Commander is. I could make all the right management choices with what I have, but if it's not in obedience to God, the supplier and owner of these resources, it doesn't really matter. On the morning of October 26, not knowing I'd be quitting my job in a couple short hours, I read from Lysa's book that *"we fear that giving sacrificially will make our lives empty, when in reality, withholding is what leads to emptiness."* I knew that if God asked for more than my tithe, it was His. I didn't know, though, that He'd ask me to give up the source from which I was tithing. I had placed conditions on my faith based on my comfort, and God tested my faith. He didn't care about the conditions of my circumstances, for He already knew the outcome. But the condition of my heart—did I trust him with the outcome?

I am not confident in quitting my job and writing this because I am a good writer, storyteller, or because my high school English teacher might read this and never take the cap off her red pen. I am not confident in this because I will be the overnight success rom-com or Instagram reel writer. I am not confident in this because it secures my future. I am not confident in this because I find my identity in the title of an author. No, I am confident in this because I am confident in the Lord, who has called me and who gives me identity and purpose. I am confident in moving forward with this because the Lord holds my future, so I will follow Him. If He tells me to throw it all away, it is trash, and my confidence will not be trashed with it. I wouldn't have said that with my past job. So if this confidence is all that comes from quitting from my job, I'll say yes to God over and over again confidently.

After I quit my job, I went home and cleaned up my apartment and organized my space for writing. I went into my closet and pulled out a box full of almost two-dozen journals. I had been writing for over five years. I started a diary in February of 2018. I was fourteen years old at that time. I wrote that I was starting a diary because I hadn't committed to my New Year's resolutions, and I wrote down what those New Year's resolutions were. I created a place of accountability for myself. One of my New Year's resolutions at fourteen years old was to "discover the meaning of life." The rest of my resolutions that year were all of the ways I figured I needed to fix myself. Since February of 2018, I have filled over eighteen physical journals, written countless notes on my iPhone, and typed out many electronic documents with short stories, ideas, poems, and even some songs. Journaling has become a huge part of my quiet time with the Lord as well. Most of my prayers are written, and it has been such a sweet way the Lord gathers my full attention. It's also been sweet to look back and see prayers of all kinds that He has answered. And in these sweet moments of writing, I'd be glad to tell fourteen-year-old me and you that the Lord has revealed to me the meaning of life. But to have that goal at fourteen years old, to discover the meaning of life, is interesting. What's more interesting is that at the same time, I was trying to find this big philosophical answer. I was also putting all my energy at fourteen years old into fixing myself. I had it *out of order*.

While I spent all my time and energy on trying to fix myself, God was at work to fix my eyes. I was not the main character. I wasn't the prodigal or the problem. My identity was out of order. This is a story of identity redemption, my story of identity redemption.

CHAPTER 2

FIRST THINGS FIRST

Whether consciously or not, we have all built an identity around something. What have you built an identity around? Perhaps it is your performance at work or at school, a sport, or a place on a team? Maybe it's in a club, a friend group, or on social media. It might even be in a relationship or in your appearance. Any of these would make sense because these are what culture tells us to find identity in. When someone says, tell me about yourself, these are the things we bring up or that speak for themselves. Who are you, though, really? I know who I am now. My story is one of identity redemption. I always associated the idea of redemption with regaining and being saved from something. Well, whether I associated the idea of redemption with that or not is actually irrelevant because that's what redemption is. Redemption is regaining something or being saved from something. Yet I never had a strong sense of identity. How can I regain something I never had? It was always seemingly misplaced and fleeting. I never knew who I was much beyond my name. I never quite fit in at school, and my mom was active-duty air force, so we moved around a good bit growing up. I faced an autoimmune disease with severe mental health issues at a young age and some abusive dynamics in my home. By the time I started to figure out what it took to be "normal" in a new place, we would move to a new normal. Yet while I was trying so hard to figure out who I was and fit in, my nervous system was in survival mode, and it felt like none of it even mattered. Maybe you can relate.

What, for a long time, was a story of pain and disorder is now my story of redemption. I was lost, but now I am found. I did regain an identity. In fact I was always identified the same in God's eyes; I just lost my identity before I knew it was mine. I hadn't realized who I was or who I was created to be. Satan thought he had me. With an enemy who steals, lies, and kills, how easy it was to steal an identity one didn't know they had, to lie about who they were with no foundation to negate it, and to kill their sense of worth and purpose. But, I'll ruin the story for you, SATAN DOESN'T WIN! This is no longer a story of pain and disorder but of redemption. This is not the sad story of a lost little girl but rather the story of a woman who knows who she is because she knows *whose* she is. My story is not my own. My story belongs to God, and it became a story of redemption and life when I surrendered it to Him, when I didn't just let go of the steering wheel but got out of the driver's seat.

I believe there is no better way to get to know yourself than to spend time with your Creator. He created you with purpose and love and intention. You were *created,* not just conceived in the physicality of your mother's womb but planned and *knitted together* so intently by God, who knows every hair on your head. You are a reflection of His creativity and were made in His image. You were designed to reflect Him. When I let go of everything I thought I might be, could be, and should be and surrendered my identity to God, I found exactly who I was created to be. I am His.

When I first got saved though, I still didn't find my identity in Christ. When we confuse what culture says and what Christ says, we get mixed messages. When we get mixed messages, we tend to rely on our own understanding. When we rely on our own understanding, we get it *out of order*. I got it out of order. I found my identity in myself as a Christian and what that title meant in my own understanding but not in Christ. Once again, I thought it was my story. I made myself the main character and the author, as culture encourages. I found my identity and worth in how "perfect" of a Christian, based on worldly definition, I could be and what others said, thought, or that I thought they might think. This was a story I wouldn't be the ultimate winner in. I found my identity and worth in making sure I could save everyone around me. This got really messy real fast if you can imagine. I didn't learn about my purpose through time *with* God, but I tried to understand it in everything I could do *for* God. I was working like a dog for the kingdom, but I wasn't listening to the King. I had good intentions and was running as fast as I could but in the wrong race. I was trying to save people instead of seeing them. I was trying to lure them in instead of just loving them. And I was taking on responsibilities God didn't give me. This is not me saying we shouldn't do things for God. No. The Bible calls us to do *all* things as if for Him. This is me saying that His love for us is not changed by our deeds; it is unconditional and never-ending. God's love is not transactional; it is unconditional. So why was I placing conditions on it for myself?—because that's what the world had shown me so far. Nothing is truly free, at least that's what I believed. But that was a lie. That was a lie meant to separate me from God's love. And God's love, freely given, is stronger, bigger, and mightier than the lies. The price has already been paid. And though I can't afford it, it is offered to me.

More than He wants anything we can do, He wants us. When I finally slowed down, somewhat by choice, somewhat by breakdown, and did less, God did more, or at least I had the time and the space to see and acknowledge all that He was already doing. He did a work in me that I was blowing off every divine appointment for before because I was too busy doing things *for* Him that I wasn't spending time *with* Him. What He wanted from me was a relationship, and I gave Him everything but that. I knew God as a Savior, but I found *my identity* when I began to know him as a friend, as a father, a provider, a comforter, a healer, a protector, my strength, my endurance, and my Lord. Because knowing him as a friend, a father, a provider, comforter, healer, a protector, my strength, my endurance, and my Lord means I am a daughter of the King, a friend of Jesus, cared for, loved, cherished, protected, safe, strong, and that I can endure tests, trials, tribulations, and temptations. These are truths.

This was not a one-day, clean-cut surrender though. This was a messy, still messy, but beautiful ongoing surrender. And how is it done?—by simply saying yes to God. There's nothing you have to do to be all that God says you are. When God created you and the plan for your life in His story, He took YOU into account—your mind, your abilities, your weaknesses, your personality, and your gifts—because He gave you each of them. You are His. He wants you, undone. He loves you, undone. He died for you, undone. He is coming back, and He has a place prepared for you, undone. Because it is already done. You are His.

Because you are His, life takes on a whole new meaning. When I first came to know Jesus, I was suicidal. I knew *of* Jesus. I got eternal life. I was baptized at a young age. I knew I was saved, but I didn't know I had purpose in living *now*. And I read, of course, the most encouraging book of the Bible at this time for a suicidal adolescent—not Psalms, not even Proverbs but what came next: Ecclesiastes. In my little brown New Living Translation Bible, Ecclesiastes, chapter 1, is titled "Everything is Meaningless." But don't worry; it gets better. There are more fun titles like "The Futility of Wisdom," "The Futility of Pleasure," "The Futility of Work," "The Futility of Political Power," "The Futility of Wealth," and even "Death Comes to All." I was suicidal when I became a Christian, and I decided, Wow, everything *is* meaningless. I set out to find the meaning of life, and I concluded that life is meaningless—that is, though, without Christ. When I realized that Christ not only matters above all else but is the reason anything else matters, a light went off for me. I wanted to drop everything and chase after Jesus, but the world quickly detoured me from that. Jesus was for eternity. I was saved, but now I'm supposed to live in the moment.

So, instead of giving my life to Jesus, instead of surrendering, I lived my life, my way, in my time, to the very best of my ability, so that at the end I could package it up all pretty, one part at a time to give to Him. And that's what I did. I took the idea of doing all things, as if for Christ and working hard and cheerfully and lived without Christ for Christ. I had it out of order. I wanted to live my life then give it to him. I wanted to get it all right. I wanted to be successful. I wanted to make it picture-perfect before I gave it to Him. I wanted to clean up the messes and hit the milestones, to give Jesus something I thought was of worth. I got it wrong. Somewhere between the light going off and the light getting buried were expectations, traumas, shame, egos, and deadlines of this world that wedged their way onto the throne that all along belonged to the Lord. I felt so lost, and that's because I had everything competing for first place. I was the Lord of my own life, subject to work, school, relationships, and all the dead-end avenues of the world. I was living for the Lord, yet I wasn't listening for Him. No matter how much I said God first, Jesus matters above all else. God's voice was not the first one I listened for when needing advice or encouragement. Jesus wasn't the first source of company I sought when needing a friend. I was saying I was living for Him, but I had it out of order. I was trying to get second things first.

My pastor shared, one morning, that you can't get second things by putting them first. You get them by putting first things first. They are second. That's just simply how it works by definition. I have learned that I am a person with all-or-nothing tendencies. Something is first, or it's last. I'm all in, or I'm all out. My music is all the way up, rattling the windows, or it's off, silent, and mute. This was fun for my parents when I was learning to drive because if I turned, I turned hard, and if I braked, with coffee inches from faces, I braked hard. And when the light went off for me, I was all in. School didn't matter. Social life didn't matter. What I did as a career didn't matter. It was all Jesus. And little by little, well-meaning youth pastors, interns, my parents, teachers, and friends began to extinguish that fire in me. I can do all things through Christ and for Christ, except for spending time with Christ and listening to Christ, because there's just no time for that. So instead of prioritizing and pursuing Christ, I began pursuing what the world had to offer, to give to

Christ. But that's not what He wanted. He wanted *me*. He wanted my heart. He died on the cross so I can have a relationship with the one I was designed after. He paid the price, and here I was, trying to give Him what He already had in His hands: the world. So when He asked me to quit my job, and the light went off for the second time since becoming a Christian, I refused to let it be dimmed again, and now you have this book.

Like I said, this is a story of identity redemption, but I want to be sure to get first things first. Jesus comes first. We are invited into His story. It is a story of redemption, but we have to remember, we are not the main character. Jesus is the main character. The whole Bible is His story. Everything in the Old Testament points to Jesus, and it's veiled until He tears the veil. We live in a generation of the New Testament and the new covenant.

A man spoke about this at my church, and he said that the Bible teaches first and foremost who God is, then second, who we are and why we exist. He preached on the statement that we must read the Bible as the real and true story of human history through the lenses of Israel. The Bible is not another self-help book or religious text. It is the word of God. God is at work through the Scripture to shape this new covenant community so we can participate in what He's up to. He wants us to be a part of it. Reading the Scripture helps us do that. It is the story of God creating a nation through which He would bless everyone. But they (Israel) started to tell themselves a different story, so they started to live according to a different story. They became the main characters and regarded God as the supporting cast. We do this. We invite God into our hearts as a supporting cast, not as the main character, not to take the throne. We consume culture's message that we are the main character and the author of our own stories, so we start writing a different story for ourselves. Then what happens when we start writing a different story for ourselves is that we start living according to our own will, our own story, instead of God's. The man preaching, Greg Dewey, said that "if we miss how our story fits into the bigger story, we end up with an individualized escapist theology." When we regard ourselves as the main character, we put God's entire purpose for us out of focus. It is through the new

IDENTITY REDEMPTION

covenant that all humans can be renewed. We read the Bible in light of it being true human history through the lens of Israel, and then we must put on the lens of the Messiah. Jesus is the ultimate and true lens of all Scripture. Greg said, "When you read the Bible through the lens of Jesus, it always gets better." This is because we get the full story. The resurrection is what tears the veil. The Old Testament was veiled until the resurrection. At the first Easter, in Luke 24, Jesus explained all the scriptures about Himself. In John 5:39–40, Jesus said, "*You search the Scriptures because you believe they give you eternal life. But the Scriptures point to me! Yet you refuse to come to me so that I can give you this eternal life.*" It's Jesus, Jesus, Jesus. Jesus is first and foremost. Jesus is not an addition for our lives but the foundation. When we read the word of God, we should think first of Jesus. What happened to Jesus is the center of events that should shape how we read all other scripture.

So then, this is God's story. Our purpose is to live in a way that points to Him, reflects Him, and represents Him. As we live our lives, we are not writing our own story but rather reading more of and seeing God's story unfold. Jesus calls us to love and love first.

> Jesus replied, "The most important commandment is this: 'Hear, O Israel! The Lord our God is the one and only Lord. And you must love the Lord your God with all your heart, all your soul, all your mind, and all your strength. The second is equally important: Love your neighbor as yourself. No other commandment is greater than these.'" (Mark 12:29–31)

So then, if loving God and loving our neighbors as ourselves is what Jesus Himself said are the greatest commandments, this, to me, makes what should come first in our lives pretty clear. Yet so often, we are distracted. Distraction gives the enemy an upper hand for destruction. What second things are you putting first? Second things aren't inherently bad they just aren't first. Sometimes it's not about what you're saying no to but what saying no makes room for.

In *The 7 Habits of Highly Effective People by Stephen R Covey*, Mr. Covey spends some time discussing time management being the management of self. He made one point that stuck with me though. He made it clear that effective people schedule their priorities; they don't prioritize their schedule. So essentially, effective people put first things first. So if loving comes first, how can we schedule that? How do we actively make love a priority?

Well, to make love a priority in our lives, we must first receive it. Second, we must make it practical. To make love a priority, we must first receive it and, second, make it practical.

To receive this love, you just say yes to God. We love because He first loved us. We don't love to get love, but rather we love because we have love. This yes is not only a receptance of this freely given love but an acknowledgment. It is an acknowledgment that while we don't *have to* earn it, we also can't earn it, and we need it. This is humbling. This makes us choose between pride and love. What will come first? This is a yes that says, "I want you. I know I fall short and am a sinner and that my sin disconnects us, but, Lord, I need You." This is a humbling yes. God wants you. He loves you. But He doesn't love sin. We are all sinners. He wants you regardless, but you have to let go of your pride, your sin, whatever it might be, to hold on to and receive His love. It requires trust, faith, humility, and sometimes a brokenhearted, end-of-yourself type of pain, but it gives hope, joy, salvation, and that love in exchange. This is a yes before you have it all together. This is a yes before you hit the milestones or clean the messes you think you should. I believe you could read every self-help book, be the most successful businesswoman, mom, sorority sister, athlete, scholar, you name it, but if you don't have love, what is it for?

> And in any event, you should desire the most helpful gifts. First, however, let me tell you about something else that is better than any of them! If I could speak in any language in heaven or on earth but didn't love others, I would only be making meaningless noise like a loud gong or a clanging cymbal. If I had the gift of prophecy,

and if I knew all the mysteries of the future and knew everything about everything, but didn't love others, what good would I be? And if I had the gift of faith so that I could speak to a mountain and make it move, without love I would be no good to anybody. If I gave everything I have to the poor and even sacrificed my body, I could boast about it; but if I didn't love others, I would be of no value whatsoever. Love is patient and kind. Love is not jealous or boastful or proud or rude. Love does not demand its own way. Love is not irritable, and it keeps no record of when it has been wronged. It is never glad about injustice but rejoices whenever the truth wins out. Love never gives up, never loses faith, is always hopeful, and endures through every circumstance. (1 Corinthians 12:31–13:1–7)

Once we choose love, once we say yes to God and receive His love, we have to make it practical. What does it actually look like to love people? What does it look like to love your neighbor as yourself? What does it look like to love your enemy? How do we prioritize a concept?—by making it a practice. To make love a priority, we have to first receive it, and then now, secondly, make it practical. Love is a priority we can't always schedule. I love the idea of scheduling our priorities, but choosing love sometimes can mean it overrides what's scheduled. Jesus discusses love in John 15 and said, *"When you obey me, you remain in my love"* (John 15:10) and that *"the greatest love is shown when people lay down their lives for their friends"* (John 15:13). I think, so often we assume that laying down our lives for our friends only means taking a bullet for our friends, being willing to die for them. But what if it's also, and mostly, being willing to give our life while we are still living? What if laying down our life for our friends is actually mostly about compromising and embodying the characteristics of love that come from the Father? What if laying down our life for our friends is actually about laying down our time, our schedules? Love is hard, no doubt.

Going back to 1 Corinthians 13, that so practically explains what love is. Love seems less—well, lovely. It actually just seems really hard and exhausting. Love is patient. Patience can be hard. Love is kind. Treating people better than we think they deserve is hard. Love is not jealous or boastful or proud. It doesn't get bitter when others get what it wants, doesn't draw attention to itself and is humble, which is hard. It's not rude. It takes into account others' feelings, which can be hard and tiring. Love does not demand its own way. It puts others' needs before its own, which is hard. Love is not irritable; it's slow to anger, which can be so hard. Love keeps no record of when it has been wronged. It doesn't get to be the victim—hard. Love does not rejoice about injustice but rejoices when the truth wins out. It never gives up ever—hard and trying. Love never loses faith; it chooses to believe the best—hard. It is always hopeful, and it sees the potential in people—hard. Love endures through every circumstance. It keeps doing all these things, even when it's hard. It's patient, kind, selfless, humble, considerate, and slow to anger. ALL. THE. TIME! Love is hard, no doubt, but we love because He first loved us. God is the source of love. He *is* love. He is patient and kind. He is considerate and slow to anger. And He loves you *regardless!* The love that we are called to, the commandment from Jesus, is not to love God *if* or even to love *because*. The commandment is not to love our neighbors as ourselves *if* or *because*. True love is love *regardless*. We are called and commanded to true love as our highest goal.

I've started reading a book that was recommended to me called *Love Your Husband Before You Even Have One* by Kim Vollendorf. Kim introduced the idea of three types of love: love *if,* love *because,* and love *regardless.* "Love *if*" is an earned love, given based on criteria met. "Love *because*" is based on a maintained quality, and "*love regardless*" is true love, not earned or always deserved, but it is a commitment. Only God is capable of making this commitment because only He can fully demonstrate all the qualities of love all the time. This is why, in order to make love a priority, we must first receive it in its truest form from the true source.

So from a God of order, we are called to love Him first, then our neighbors as ourselves. So when we read our Bibles, how we take care of ourselves, how we work, how we cook, clean, train, talk, and live, we should put love first. This means there is ministry in the mundane. To practice receiving it, we have to familiarize ourselves with the voice of God. How can we say yes to a voice we don't recognize? Scheduling time to be in the word of God and prioritizing quiet time with Him is essential so that when you're busy, and you're running late for work, and He asks you to quit your job, you can recognize His voice. So that when it's time to lay your life down for your friends, you have a guide and full cup to pour from. But when love comes first, what comes second? When we put God first and are willing to obey, to love *regardless* of our schedules, feelings, thoughts, and opinions, what comes second?

Surely, our careers, our families, the load of laundry or six loads, what to make for dinner, the assignment we have due, the event we have scheduled, our health, and all of these things that fill our time—surely they matter. They do! But when you put first things first love, how they matter changes. What they mean can be different because who you are and your worth is no longer attached to them. You're not living for them. These things change because you've changed.

When you accept God's love, it makes you new. When you've put love first, what's for dinner might change. How the laundry gets put away might change. The way you complete that assignment or even just talk to others around you should change. When you put first things first, they should reflect in what's second. This is our whole purpose: to reflect the Lord and His love! To fulfill our purpose, we must put Jesus first.

We often are told, as Christians, the narrative of inviting Jesus into your heart to become a Christian, to get saved. I understand the point of this narrative to illustrate the choice given, but I think, really, we are invited into *His story*. A pastor of mine once explained that the Bible is actually His story. We are invited into *His* story. Our choice is whether or not we yield to it. Accepting Christ's love and making Him the Lord of our life means our life now yields to Him as do second things yield to first things. We're not inviting Him to tag along in our plans, but we're choosing to yield to His plans. What you do second is important, but it's not the most important thing. When you put first things first, you do everything else as a result of this priority. The cool thing about getting first things first is when your story begins. When you're yielding to God, what's second for you might not be second for someone else. But remember, you can't get second things by putting them first.

Have you ever tried to put second things first? You try so hard to get something right (just like you saw on Pinterest?), and it just doesn't work out, or you try to make the relationship work, but it's just not. So then you start praying like, "Please, God, don't let me have wasted my afternoon on this recipe," or "Please, God, don't let me be in a relationship with the wrong person," "Please change them." But you can't get second things by putting them first. When you put first things first, when you put God first, you might notice you spend more time praying for preparation and planning rather than spending your time pleading with God.

The first is typically the beginning of something. With God, every time you put Him first, you are made new.

> That is why we never give up. Though our bodies are dying, our spirits are being renewed every day." (2 Corinthians 4:16)

For me, what came second, what began, was a story of identity redemption. I tried so long to get second things first, even after becoming a Christian. I put second things first in my relationship with God by trying to put the fruits before Him. I was trying to follow all the rules. I was trying to love people. I was trying to forgive. I was trying to be honest. I was trying to be kind. I was trying to be patient. And I was dying trying. This supposed to be life-giving thing was killing me. But I thought, *Man, I am dying for the Lord. I am such a good Christian. And yet I'm still falling short, and reading my Bible is just exhausting.* I was trying. I was spending all of this time and this energy and was so, so busy trying that I wasn't listening. I wasn't following. I was trying before I became a Christian, and I was trying after. Nothing really changed. I was reading the Bible like a self-help book, like I was the main character, trying to see where I fit and how I could be better and was just *trying* to be a Christian. I was looking through the lens of the media's aesthetic of "that girl" instead of the heart of His girl. It felt hopeless. But being a Christian is not about all this trying. Being a Christian is about following. It is not about trying to hold it all together but about laying it all down. It is not about perfection but about proximity to the Lord.

We are followers of Christ. When we are called into positions of leadership, it's not because *we* are leading but because we are *following* Him into it. Our efforts follow suit with our following. We no longer have to try and figure it all out; we just have to trust. We don't have to change anything to become a Christian; Christ transforms us through our surrender. When my heart posture changed to a state of surrender, and I got first things first, the second things were better than I could have ever imagined. Now this is not another prosperity gospel, saying if you accept God's love and surrender to Him, your life will be sunshine and rainbows. This is not a transaction but a transformation. This is the good news, the gospel, that our freedom, our joy, our peace, our hope, and our source of life are no longer dependent on all the second things. Christ paid it all.

So like I said, my story is one of identity redemption, or rather my part in His story is. My story is not one I could have written or orchestrated on my own. I have a tattoo on my wrist that says *faith*. This tattoo is in my own handwriting, and I got it when I turned eighteen. However, the *i* in *faith* is replaced with a semicolon. In case you aren't familiar with the symbolism of a semicolon, a semicolon represents a sentence that an author could have chosen to end but chose not to. The original meaning of the semicolon tattoo is that you are the author, and the sentence is your life. It represents a struggle with suicidal ideation. However, replacing the *i* in *faith* (which also happens to be my middle name) is my symbol of surrendering the rest of my story to God. My "fa;th" tattoo is a symbol of my testimony. It is a symbol that I wouldn't not just kill myself but surrender the rest of my story to God, declaring that He was the author, not me. For two years, I wrestled with this surrender that I declared at eighteen years old. Little did I know this tattoo would be the cover of my book two years later and a testament to my story of identity redemption the Lord was writing. Surrendering my life to God saved my life and redeemed my identity.

CHAPTER 3

THIS IS GOD'S STORY

As I am recalling my story of identity redemption, I can't help but think about Joseph of the Old Testament's story in the Bible. It never dawned on me the importance of family and lineage until I realized that in nearly every story, there is family. I always skipped past the lists of hard-to-pronounce biblical names and never paid much attention. I was never drawn to the long historical facts, nor was I the one to be connecting all the dots until I realized just how awe-striking this story truly is when you do. I am drawn to the story of Joseph. I knew the elementary version that Joseph was the youngest brother, and he was the favorite, and his brothers couldn't stand him. When Joseph got this special robe, I remember it as a striped, rainbow, thick cardigan because that was the prop we had in Sunday school as a child. His brothers were jealous as all-get-out. As the cherry-on-top to their jealousy sundae, Joseph told them about his dreams of their bundles of grain bowing down to his bundles of grain. So they planned to kill him. But they didn't want to be responsible for his death, so they decided they'd leave him in a pit to die. How nice of them. Before they left him there for good though, they saw tradesmen coming and had the brilliant idea to sell their brother, Joseph, to be the tradesmen's slave and allow their father to assume Joseph got eaten by an animal in the fields that day. But despite their plans for evil, God made Joseph's dreams come true, and he became a great leader in Egypt. During the famine years later, Joseph's brothers came to him for grain and bowed down to him, not realizing who he was. Joseph blessed them, and they become a great nation. I suppose the lesson ingrained in me from the third-grade level is that good always wins out in the end, and God's plan prevails.

While that lesson is good, I never understood the deeper value in this story, and I'm sure there is more I still don't understand or notice yet. What I do notice now though is who Joseph's father was. The fact that Joseph even existed is proof of God's higher-arching plan. In Joseph's story, it blows my mind that from this line of descendants, Jesus would also be born.

But Joseph's father, Jacob, was a con man in his youth. He deceived his brother to take his birthright and then lied about who he was to receive his father's, Isaac's, blessing instead of his older brother, Esau. Esau hated Jacob for this and planned to kill him once his father died. So even in the Old Testament, we see wars come to be from family disputes. When Esau and Jacob were born, it was said that they would be rival nations. From the family line that Jesus would be born into this world to, we see brothers said to be leaders of rival nations. Well, Esau's plans to kill him were found out, and Jacob fled until Esau could chill out and not be so angry that he literally wanted to kill him.

Jacob was gone, and he'd been blessed abundantly while starting his family, and he sent back for Esau years later. He was hoping he'd be friendly and referred to himself as Esau's servant. Well, Esau went on his way to Jacob with an army of four hundred men. He and his army were likely not feeling too friendly. Jacob divided his household, thinking that whichever one Esau would attack, he'd get away with the other. And in the meantime, he was praying to God about his faithfulness and love that He had shown him already through his blessings.

Jacob put a present together for Esau, still hoping he'd be friendly. As Jacob finally approached his brother, he bowed before him seven times, and Esau actually embraced him affectionately. What an example of forgiveness! It was a very positive exchange, and he showed him his family and flocks and herds. Esau didn't want to accept the gifts from Jacob, saying that he already had plenty, and their exchange makes me chuckle just a bit because they went back and forth, like two friends fighting over who's paying for lunch. Esau had some of his men guide Jacob and protect him. Jacob made it back to the land of his father and had, in his old age, an eleventh son named Joseph. Without the element of forgiveness and grace in this family's line, Joseph's story wouldn't be. God blessed both brothers and was faithful in their time of disconnect.

And then, looking back just one more generation to Joseph's grandfather, Jacob's father, Isaac, who, if you know the story, was the son of Abraham, was almost sacrificed. God told Abraham and Sarah, Isaac's mother, that a great nation would come from their son. Isaac was their one and only son. Sarah was barren before the time she gave birth to Isaac, which is just another great story. I'm telling you, the Bible is the best drama you'll ever read. So then, their one and only son, a gift, fulfilled promise, and answered prayer, God told Abraham to take to the top of a mountain and kill as a sacrifice for Him. Holy moly! But Abraham obeyed and took Isaac to this mountain. Isaac was like, "Dad, where's our sacrifice?" which is so awkward. And before Abraham would kill Isaac, an angel appeared to tell him not to harm him. The angel told him he knew he feared the Lord and not to harm Isaac. So Isaac was off the hook, and God was happy with Abraham. Well, fast-forward to Joseph, Isaac's grandson, and here is the story that really catches my attention.

Once Joseph was sold as a slave to the tradesmen, we see a few twists and turns in his story. His worth, at this point, from the world was twenty pieces of silver. That is what his brothers sold him for. But then, an officer of Pharaoh, the king of Egypt, named Potiphar, purchased him for a value I don't know. Potiphar was the captain of the palace guard, and he recognized that the Lord was with Joseph. So Joseph received God's favor with Potiphar and was put in charge of Potiphar's household and his business dealings. The Lord blesses Potiphar for his treatment of Joseph, and this blessing prompted Potiphar to give Joseph total administrative responsibility. Things were looking up for Joseph, the boy sold for twenty pieces of silver to traders.

This was until Potiphar's wife invited Joseph to sleep with her. Joseph said no, reasoning that that would be against God. She pressured him every day, and he just avoided her. Well, one day, she grabbed him by the shirt and demanded that he sleep with her. She was not good with rejection, clearly, and he ran. But as he ran from her, she tore his shirt. As he had fled, she screamed and started yelling that he was trying to rape her. When Potiphar, her husband, returned home, she told him her story. She claimed that her screaming saved her. Potiphar, understandably so, was pissed and put Joseph in prison.

But the Lord's favor was also with Joseph in prison. He gained favor with the chief jailer, who put him in charge of the prison, and the Lord, with him, made everything run smoothly and successfully. Pharaoh, while Joseph was in prison, put two officials in prison: his chief cupbearer and chief baker. They remained in prison for a long time, and Potiphar assigned Joseph to take care of them. These two officials had dreams they didn't know the meaning of, and so they went to Joseph for interpretation. He informed them that interpreting dreams is God's business as they told him their dreams. To the cupbearer, Joseph explained that his dream meant that after three days, Pharaoh would take him and return him to his position as chief cupbearer. Joseph asked that when he did return to his position that he would have pity and mention him to Pharaoh to let him out. To the chief baker, Joseph told him that his dream meant that Pharaoh would cut off his head and impale his body on a pole and that birds would come to peck at his flesh. Yikes. Three days passed, and it happened to be Pharaoh's birthday, and both of the dreams became reality, just as Joseph said. The cu-bearer, though, forgot about Joseph and didn't mention him. It actually says that he gave it no thought. This seems like something that would be hard to give no thought.

IDENTITY REDEMPTION

So two years passed, and now Pharaoh was having dreams that nobody had been able to interpret for him. Finally, the cupbearer remembered Joseph and told Pharaoh about him. Pharaoh ordered him in. Joseph got clean clothes, a fresh shave, and said that interpreting dreams was beyond his power but that God could tell him what it meant. Joseph interpreted Pharaoh's dream and told him it meant there would be seven years of prosperity, followed by seven years of famine and that he suggested putting the wisest man in charge of a nationwide program to collect a fifth of the crops during the good years so there would be enough during the famine. Pharaoh appointed Joseph to this position, saying that he was obviously a man filled with the spirit of God. He gave Joseph his signet ring as a sign of his authority, as well as nice clothes and a gold chain. He gave him his second-command chariot, and everywhere he went, people were commanded to bow down to him. So Joseph went from being sold into slavery to being a prisoner, accused of rape, to being dripped out and in charge of all of Egypt. Wow. Pharaoh declared that he was still king but that nothing could be done in Egypt without Joseph's approval.

Pharaoh gave Joseph a wife, who happened to be the daughter of Potiphar, which I think is so funny and ironic. They spent the seven years of prosperity, collecting grain, and their stores were overflowing. During this time, they had two sons. When the famine hit, Pharaoh directed people to Joseph, the only one selling grain. The famine was widespread, and Jacob, Joseph's father (who thought he'd been dead this whole time), heard there was grain in Egypt and sent Joseph's ten older brothers to buy some. He had had a twelfth son, Benjamin but didn't want him going because of what happened long ago with Joseph.

Joseph was now the governor of Egypt, and when his brothers arrived, he recognized them but pretended to be a stranger. They bowed before him, but he accused them of being spies. They promised they were honest men and told Joseph how there were twelve of them, one no longer with them and one youngest brother at home. Joseph said he would test them and swore by the life of Pharaoh that they would not leave Egypt unless they brought back their younger brother to prove they were honest men. He told them to send one brother to get him while he kept the rest of them there bound in prison. So they were in prison for three days. Then Joseph said that he was a God-fearing man, and if they did as he said, they would live. He said, "Only one of you will remain in prison, while the rest, go home with grain for your families." He said to "still bring your youngest back to me" so that he knew if they were telling the truth and that if they were, he would spare them. They all decided this was because of what they did to Joseph years ago when they saw his terror and anguish and pleadings and didn't listen. They were speaking among themselves without realizing that Joseph was standing there and that he understood. Joseph left the room to wept at this point. He returned and chose Simeon and tied him up before their eyes. He ordered his servants to fill their sacks with grain but to also secretly return their payments to them at the top of their sacks.

They returned to their father and told him everything and dumped out all their sacks of grain. Scripture says that terror gripped them when they realized each bag had all their money. Jacob was upset saying he was deprived of his children because Joseph disappeared, Simeon was gone now, and now they wanted to take Benjamin. He said everything was going against him. They reasoned and pleaded with their father. When they never got any relief from the famine, Jacob told his sons to go and buy more grain. They warned that the man (Joseph) wasn't joking when he said not to return without Benjamin, their youngest brother. They reasoned that they would either all die of starvation or they would take Benjamin. So they went, and Jacob said to get the best products of the land, take the man gifts, take double the money he returned in their sacks, and he prayed for God to give them mercy.

When they got to Egypt, and Joseph saw Benjamin with them, he asked the manager of his household to organize a feast for them and to take them to his palace. His brothers were so scared as to where they were going. Keep in mind, they were fearful, and they still didn't even realize this was Joseph. They assumed that this man was planning to pretend that they stole the money, seize them as slaves, and take their donkeys. They told the household manager about the money, who told them to relax and not to worry, and that it must have been God because they collected their money all right. They got to the palace and prepared their gifts for Joseph. Joseph came, and they bowed before him. Joseph asked about his father, and they bowed again. He asked about Benjamin, if this was the younger brother, and he prayed God's grace over him. Joseph got overcome by emotion for his brother and left quickly to cry. During the feast, he ate by himself, and his brothers were at a separate table. He seated his brothers in order from oldest to youngest, which just amazed them because they still didn't realize who this man they were feasting with was. They were served from Joseph's table, and he gave Benjamin five times more than anyone else. As they were getting ready to leave, he had their sacks filled with grain, and again, their money returned. He said to put his silver cup in the top of the younger brother's sack.

The brothers set out, but Joseph sent his household manager out for them to ask why they repaid kindness for evil, why they'd stolen his personal cup, which he used to predict the future. His brothers were like, "What do you mean? What kind of men do you think we are?" like, "We brought back the money. So they told him, "If you find this cup with any of us, you can let that one die, and the rest of us will be your master's slaves forever." They were confident. His household manager replied to them and said, "Just the one who stole it will be a slave, and the rest of you can go free." So they found the cup in Benjamin's sack and tear their clothing in despair and returned to the city. Joseph was home, and they fell before him. Joseph asked what they were trying to do and said, "Don't you know that a man, such as I, would know who stole it?" They were asking how they could plead and prove their innocence, saying that God was punishing them for their sins and said that they had all returned to be his slaves. Joseph said, "No. Go home. Only the man who stole the cup will be my slave." They pleaded with him and told him about their father not wanting Benjamin to go and how his life was bound up in this boy's life and that if he saw he was not with them, he would die. Joseph couldn't stand it and broke down and cried that he was Joseph. He told them he was Joseph, who they sold. He told them not to be angry with themselves because God did it and sent him there ahead of time to preserve their lives. He said he was there to keep them and their families alive so they would become a great nation. He kept reiterating that God sent him there, not them.

He sent them back to their father and called them all to live in Egypt, where he would take care of them because there were still five more years of famine to come. He told them to tell their father about how he'd been honored in Egypt, and he embraced Benjamin, still crying. He kissed each of his brothers. When Pharaoh got news that these were Joseph's brothers, he was happy and told them to bring their father and all their families, and they'd get the best territory in Egypt. On the way there, God spoke to Jacob in a vision and told him not to be afraid and that it'd be a great nation, that He was with him but that he'd die in Egypt with Joseph. So they went, sixty-six descendants in total, with all of their livestock and belongings, to Egypt. They arrived, and Joseph and his father embraced and, as you can imagine, wept. Keep in mind, this was over ten years later—ten years of Jacob thinking Joseph was gone forever.

Joseph bought all of Egypt's land for Pharaoh because people were selling it out of need for food. Jacob lived there for seventeen years and had Joseph make an oath to bury him with his ancestors, not in Egypt. Jacob blessed Joseph's sons before he died. Once Jacob died, Joseph's brothers assumed he actually wanted revenge on them. So they told him that before Jacob died, he told them to tell Joseph to forgive them, and then they bowed before him and said they were now his slaves. Joseph told them not to be afraid because he wasn't God to judge or punish them.

> As far as I am concerned, God turned into good what you meant for evil. He brought me to the high position I have today so I could save the lives of many people. (Genesis 50:20)

He said that he'd take care of them and their families. He lived to see three generations of his descendants and told his brothers, before he died, that God would come for them and lead them out of Egypt into the land he vowed.

Since the times of the Old Testament, before Jesus was born to this world, God has been working in families. He designed family. We make things really messy. We get selfish, and we get jealous. We have the same flesh that Joseph's brothers operated in when they sold him into slavery. But we get to serve the same God, whose favor made Joseph the leader of nations and whose mercy and grace made him the caretaker of his family, the family that sold him into slavery. We have to be reminded that God is at the center of family, or we go off the line and sell each other short and sell each other out. Even if your mother, father, their mothers and fathers, your brother, sister, aunts, and uncles don't follow Jesus, you can, and you get to. And like Joseph said, you are not God to judge them. You are in the family you are in for a reason, the same reason Isaac was born to Sarah and Abraham, wasn't sacrificed after all, that Jacob was born to Isaac, Joseph to Jacob, and all of Joseph's brothers. This is all part of a much bigger story—God's story. Further down the line, Jesus would come into the family's lineage and this great nation, but through Him would come an even greater nation: the kingdom of God.

But even in just the story of Joseph, there is so much to unpack, and there is much revealed about the character of God. The same God of Abraham, Isaac, Jacob, and Joseph is the same God of the kingdom coming we serve today. The same God who was with Joseph is with me and wants to be with each of us. There are a few things I find interesting about Joseph in this story. Even as he had been sold as a slave, was working for a Roman officer as a servant, and had been thrown in jail, it is obvious to others that God was with him. It is obvious he was filled with the Spirit. I can only assume this is because he bore the fruit of the Spirit and was reflecting God's character. When Paul, later in the Bible, discussed the fruit of the Spirit, it is nine characteristics that have also been referred to as the fruit of God's character. So even when he was sold out, accused, imprisoned, and forgotten, he was fulfilling His purpose, reflecting the Lord. I notice his faithfulness. It could have been very easy when Potiphar's wife began coming on to him that he could have thought he deserved some pleasure or even liked the attention for once, but he avoided her because it was against God. When he was imprisoned and got the opportunity to interpret dreams for Pharaoh's officers, he gave the glory to God and was humble. When he was forgotten *for years* but finally stood before Pharaoh to interpret his dreams, he didn't even hesitate to give God the glory. The humility of Joseph is hard to miss. But then, as Joseph was in his high position, and his brothers had come before him, I can't help but wonder about the emotions he'd overcome with and wrestled with. The Word says he was overcome with emotion, but I don't know for certain if it is anger, sadness, bitterness. grief, joy, relief, or happiness. He broke down, and he cried so hard that he could be heard through the palace before he revealed himself to his brothers. I picture him framing Benjamin with the silver cup and wonder if he saw a chance at revenge but couldn't do it. The brothers stuck to their story that their brother was torn to pieces by animals, even to Joseph. Did the Holy Spirit direct him against his flesh? God was with Joseph, and he was filled with the Spirit, though still a human. I can't imagine the spiritual warfare experienced in these moments.

    He probably could have paid his brothers back and been justified in doing so. He could have taken revenge on the new brother. He was sold into slavery, sold as a servant, accused, imprisoned, and forgotten, and yet the Lord protected his heart, and he committed to caring for them and their families. The Lord never left him. When Joseph never condemned his brothers for what they did to him, it caught me off guard and convicted me. I thought, *This is not how this should end.* He cared for them? This is no story of justice. But the veil was not torn yet. The nation that comes from this points to a much greater coming—the coming of the Messiah and the coming of the kingdom of God. This story is a part of a story so much bigger than just Joseph, his brothers, and the nation coming in Egypt. This is about the kingdom of heaven to come.

    Joseph's story doesn't really feel like a story of justice, but truth wins out. Sure, Joseph's brothers did bow down to him in the end, but after all they did to him and all that happened as a result, for Joseph to not be bitter shows me love. I get this overwhelming sense of peace for Joseph toward the end of this story that I can really only explain, at this point, to be the peace that comes from God. I think so often, we want peace, but in reality, we want closure, or we want our idea of justice or even revenge. We want to know that someone is sorry for what they've done. I bet Joseph's therapist would have encouraged him to set boundaries with his family and, while not seeking revenge, also not needing to care for them. But when we get first things first, the care we give for others, the love we show, and the peace we behold don't come from our circumstances.

Joseph knew his identity because he knew God was with him. He knew he wasn't God, and that distinction is important. I can't say this for a fact, but I don't think Joseph spent all his time *trying* to bear good fruit but spent more time *with* the vine from which we could bear good fruit. If it was obvious that God was with Joseph and that Joseph was filled by the Holy Spirit, I am going to assume he bore good fruit: love, joy, peace, patience, kindness, gentleness, goodness, faithfulness, and self-control. And since these are the fruit of God's character, we see more of who God is through what He had done with Joseph. We see his patience as he was forgotten for years and his faithfulness after all that time when he presented before Pharaoh; it is obvious he was Spirit-filled. We see the love that keeps no record of wrongs or boasts and his kindness, gentleness, and goodness to bless and care for his brothers and their families. We see Joseph's self-control to resist temptation with Potiphar's wife and to resist revenge with Benjamin and his brothers. I just wonder what Joseph's joy looked like that made it *obvious* the Lord was with him. And yet these things came second. When I read this story, I know my younger self would have thought, *Okay, so I need to care for others, even if I don't think they deserve it, know that God is in control and turns evil for good, be patient, and faithful.* I would have seen where I connected with Joseph, made myself the main character, and turned this into a self-help book. I don't need to be more like Joseph but more like Jesus. Joseph was kind and patient and faithful because he walked with the Lord. The fruit is second to the vine. Jesus said in John 15:4, *"Remain in me, and I will remain in you. For a branch cannot produce fruit if it is severed from the vine, and you cannot be fruitful apart from me."* This is about being *with* God. It's not about trying to be like

Him but to be with Him. We become like who we spend time with, inevitably.

Our identities can't come from our circumstances. I imagine the different ways this could play out if Joseph found his identity in his circumstances or if he got peace from closure and based his treatment of his family off their treatment of him. How would Joseph have acted if he took on the identity of a slave or a prisoner? From a young age, he believed God had destined him for greatness. God assured him of a position of leadership over his parents and brothers, but the path he came to that position probably didn't look like what he dreamed of and was promised. Yet God was with him. I know the same God who was with Joseph is with me, and I have placed my identity in him. I am His daughter. He has a purpose for my life. I am in the family I am in for a reason. My circumstances do not define my identity. The same God that was with Joseph in slavery and in prison is the same God that was with him in his high position over Egypt and his blessings. This is the same God that is with me and is inviting you to be with Him.

You are wanted by Him. The Lord wants nothing more than to be with us. He doesn't want our perfection. He handled that by paying the price for our sin on the cross. He rose from the grave and defeated the stronghold of sin so we can be *with* Him. He wanted to be with Joseph and with Joseph's brothers. And yet, though he is a jealous God, He is jealous for you, and He gives you the choice. You can choose all the second things and try to do it your own way and get second things first, or you can choose Him, yield to Him, put Him first, and surrender second things for better things. I am not saying that if you put God first, the house you live in will improve or the car you drive will be better. But when you put God first and yield to His story, your heart changes, and that's what makes the second things better. When you put God first, you trust that He knows what's better and actually best for you. I was singing in worship, one afternoon, before writing, and I was singing that "Something always changes when I bless your name," and I just said, "My heart, Lord. My circumstances don't always change when I choose You, when I bless Your name, but my heart does. Thank You." You're no longer looking to second things to fill your cup because when you put God first, He is more than enough. And even when you have nothing, your cup is overflowing. It's not something, I admit, that makes sense until you know it and experience God for yourself.

CHAPTER 4

GOD, WHERE WERE YOU?

I was unlike Joseph for a long time. I found identity in circumstances for so long, though I didn't so much as identify with my circumstance or what people said about me as much as I tried to prove I *wasn't* my circumstances. I tried everything to have control. Instead of being *with* God, I tried to be *for* God. I tried really hard to be a Christian and didn't understand what came first following Jesus. I embraced the fruit of the Spirit but not the Holy Spirit. I was trying to be like Jesus more than I was trying to be with Him, which is backward. Eventually, I found myself lost in the trying and was just frankly exhausted. I figured I'd find myself and be happy in what's *next*. I have been on defense mode most of my life. But when I let go of everything, I thought I should be. I not only realized who I could be but who I was made to be. This came second to getting to know God, my Creator. We are made in His image and in His likeness, so the best way to find yourself, as people say your twenties are great for, is to find Jesus. Seek out the Lord. The good news is that He's never stopped seeking and pursuing you and your heart.

The same God that was with Joseph is the same God with me today. Joseph's story didn't feel like one of justice. It doesn't seem like the playing field was made level, yet he cared for the same brothers that sold him into slavery. I can understand a fraction of what Joseph may have felt as he was given this dream and this vision but then sold into slavery. When he gained authority but then was accused and imprisoned and when he was forgotten but then had great power, he could have become prideful in proving everyone wrong, like I did. He could have sought revenge. He could have left his family in the famine, like they left him, and unwelcomed them according to his boundaries, like I would have. But the Lord was with him. He forgave, and he cared. And while it doesn't look like forgiveness and justice truly go together, they do. Love loves justice, and love loves when the truth wins out. Just as the price has been paid for my sins, so the price has been paid for those who have sinned against me. So just as the Lord had grace and favor for Joseph, He had grace and favor for Joseph's brothers, the guys who I wouldn't think deserve it. I find it so interesting of God to deliver grace through the man they disgraced. God never left Joseph, but He also never left Joseph's brothers. He had been there through it all. So I found myself looking back at my own story and asking, "God, where were you?" I looked back for so long, struggling to see where God was in my story beyond whether or not I was going to heaven or hell and realized that it's hard to recognize where somebody is if you don't know who somebody is. In asking this question, "God, where were you?" God has shown me not only where He was but more so *who* he was, is, and will always be. This is how He redeemed my identity.

Before I hit puberty, I got diagnosed with PANS/ PANDAS. If you don't know what that is, it stands for pediatric acute-onset neuropsychiatric syndrome (PANS)/pediatric autoimmune neuropsychiatric disorder associated with streptococcal (PANDAS)—a mouthful, I know. PANS is a neuropsychiatric condition, which is triggered by a misdirected immune response to an unknown trigger, causing inflammation in the brain, leading to both physical and psychiatric symptoms. It means that the common cold, mold exposure, or a sunburn can be a living hell for a little girl. PANDAS is a subset of PANS. It's triggered by a misdirected immune response, not to an unknown trigger but to streptococcal. Symptoms can appear while the infection is still present or several months later. It usually starts with an acute onset of obsessive-compulsive disorder and/or tics and/or eating restrictions. It can also include anxiety, loss of skills, psychosis, intrusive thoughts, irritability, hyperactivity, sleep disturbances, mood swings, and urinary problems. PANS/PANDAS affects one in two hundred children, and I always thought, *Why me, God?* I wonder if Joseph ever asked that same question when he was enslaved, imprisoned, and forgotten.

I was a fun-loving, messy child, who, overnight, became a little girl threatening to kill herself and her mother. That's not the sentence chosen for dramatics but rather the mellow, chalked-up summary. I had an intense, severe, and acute onset of anxiety that nothing was clean enough and had compulsions to get everything perfect. It was extreme and made me completely irrational. Another girl with PANDAS wrote in her story that "my OCD would make me disinfect the house over and over and have rage attacks when things got 'contaminated' in my mind." All I knew at my young age was that this feeling was awful, but if I just leaned into the intrusive thoughts and compulsions, I temporarily felt better. My brain felt like it was on fire. Anyone who got in the way of my relief became an enemy in a way. While my mother was trying to help me by reassuring me things were clean (and if you know my mom, you know she keeps a ridiculously clean home), I, in that state, saw her as trying to keep me from relief. I don't remember all the things I would say, but I know that in these episodes, I hurt the people I loved, mostly my mother, my safe place. That first night, my parents called the cops on me, and my dad was ready to send me to juvie. Anything he threatened to make me behave, I would respond, "I don't care." He couldn't hit me hard enough. Grounding didn't work. I was willing to lose anything for a moment of relief. I remember genuinely wanting to die. I remember my dad getting angrier and angrier with me and my feeling completely helpless. However, the officer that night advised my parents that he thought this was medical, not just a behavior issue.

So the next morning, we went to the emergency room, and at age eleven, I was admitted to a psychiatric hospital in September of 2015. At the hospital, they tested for strep. And while I didn't present with any typical symptoms, I was positive for strep and began antibiotics. Within twenty-four hours on antibiotics, I was back to my normal, healthy self and didn't understand why I was in the hospital with these other children and adults (who thought that was a good idea?) acting in ways I couldn't dare to imagine I fit in with twenty-four hours prior. *I don't belong here*, I thought. I'd sit in group sessions thinking, *I'm not like them. Am I? Am I crazy?* My identity was up in the air, and everyone had something different to say about who I was and, more importantly to them, what was wrong with me. Traumatized feels like a dramatic, trigger-happy word in this day and age, but this hospital stay traumatized me.

The good news is that with PANS/PANDAS, 95 percent of patients outgrow the condition as they reach their adult years and past puberty, and their immune systems mature. Many, though, can face permanent brain damage from the condition, and I am so thankful that was not my case. The rage episodes came and went for years, but as I recovered postpuberty, I tried to figure out who I was. At the time that I would begin to form an identity beyond just my name and eye color, I was thrown into crisis. I would spend the next few years, trying to fix myself, even after I recovered from my disorder. I developed a fundamental belief that love was earned, and I didn't measure up in any way. I carried a lot of shame for the things I said and did as a child in these episodes. There was no way to undo anything that had happened, so I had to fix myself and beat the odds.

This was about the same time my mom retired from the air force, my dad would go from being a stay-at-home dad to working again, and our family would move halfway across the country. I was also, of course, in puberty, a fun time in and of itself. My mom often got the short end of the stick with my PANDAS episodes because I could let my guard down around her, so our relationship was tense beyond the typical teenage mom-daughter angst. There was a lot of transition and tension for my family at this time. I couldn't trust my dad, couldn't stand my mom, and I felt like an outcast in social situations because for so long I was just in survival mode. My memories of middle and high school are pretty much a blur. The high levels of stress and trauma placed me into survival mode, so all my energy was put into surviving during that time. My dad became abusive toward mostly me and my mother and pounded it into my head that many parents of kids with PANS/PANDAS divorced. He told me all the things I was, would always be, and could never be. Anything I did in a PANS/PANDAS episode was another marker of my identity. Shame and humility were to be synonymous for me. I was the reason he did and said the things he did. I was the reason their marriage was on the rocks. So I took on all the guilt, all the shame, and tried to be perfect in every way to save him, save my mom, save their marriage, and save my family. I compared myself in every way to what I thought I should be. I knew that it wasn't my fault I had PANS/PANDAS, and I couldn't have known better as a child how to react to it and cope, especially since I had no example for how to healthily deal with emotions. I took on the responsibilities to fix everything.

    I wanted control and knew that I couldn't directly control the people around me, but I could control myself. I spent my time analyzing everything wrong with me. I looked in the mirror and tried to fix what I saw first, which led to struggling with disordered eating for years. As I was on the cusp of recovery, my struggle with bulimia landed me in the hospital again as the medicine for my PANS/PANDAS didn't work if I was throwing it up. This just became another thing to hide because once again, I caused more anger in my family. By the time high school came, I figured, if I was going to hurt, I would rather hurt physically and struggled with self-harm. I tried to be perfect and prove, mostly my dad, wrong. I knew I was saved for eternal life, but I was just getting by in this life. God met my needs in this time with outlets, like the gym, some friends I had, and more. Though I didn't recognize Him, He was there. I became obsessed with the gym though and relied on it to save/fix myself and avoid my life as I knew it.

IDENTITY REDEMPTION

My last year of high school, I worked five part-time jobs while being a full-time student. I began dating an older guy I shouldn't have, graduated high school, and got the job to start making some real money. I was also studying to become a personal trainer and nutrition coach, as well as working Sundays and Wednesdays at my church as a children's Bible teacher. I was doing it, I thought. I was building a life for myself. I was making good money. People saw someone strong and successful, and that's even what I saw in the mirror. I was full of pride though and had no idea how to be soft or let my guards down. If you asked me how I was, I'd have told you I was busy. I had no idea *how* I was or even *who* I was, but I was busy being it. I had no idea how to let go of anything, and eventually, you can only carry so much. I left the guy (a whole other soap-opera story), moved out of my parent's house. And as I came out of survival mode, the years of trauma hit me, so I did what I did best—avoided it and tried to go back into survival mode. God had a different plan for who I'd be though.

I prided myself on being strong, but God wanted to use my weaknesses. I started a podcast and shared my testimony of how "God met me at the squat rack." My podcast was a "nobody cares, work harder" Christian podcast. It was a self-improvement podcast. It was well-intentioned but not what God was asking me to do. He wasn't asking me to improve my life but surrender it. I wanted what sounded good and felt good to me, but that wasn't what God had for me. I was a personal trainer, insurance producer, studying to be a nutrition coach, and a children's Bible teacher. And if you ever listened to my podcast, you'd have heard, "And more to come." Little did I know that "more to come" meant I'd actually start taking on less of the titles I thought noteworthy to my identity. I would stop personal training. Then I would stop my podcast. Then I would stop teaching Sunday school. Then I would start therapy, and then I would eventually become unemployed (cue the sparkle emojis. If you know, you know). The more I opened up my schedule, the more God opened up my eyes, and the more I began to heal. I found myself lost without these titles and realized that I didn't really know who I was. I began to receive the love I was trying so desperately to earn. I got a grace from God and experienced true freedom. I didn't have to beat the odds. Jesus already won.

Who I thought I was, all the love I thought I had to earn, and everything I thought I had to fix—God was asking me to lay down. He wanted to redeem my identity. He had more for me than shame and guilt. He had a purpose for my life greater than the responsibilities I took on for myself. I didn't have to prove anyone wrong. God made me for a purpose, and who He made to be would not be compromised by a diagnosis, abuse, or my own understanding. I sang a song in high school, "Build My Life." Maybe you've heard it? But it sings that *"I will build my life upon your love. It is a firm foundation."* I sang this for years in my trying. When we think of building, we think of hammer and nails, of making something, of putting things together. But a foundation comes first. God wanted to strip down everything I believed so far about who He was, who I was, and my life's purpose. He wanted to make a new foundation. One of the verses I prayed, not knowing the ways God would move in my life, was "open up my eyes in wonder and show me who you are. Fill me with your heart, and lead me in your love to those around me." God has opened up my eyes and shown me who He is. He has given me a new foundation and is filling me with His heart.

God drew me back to my family through quitting my job to write a book. When He told me to quit my job to write the book, I didn't realize He would be opening my eyes to parts of His story I've missed by thinking I was the main character. This was the last layer to break down to reach the foundation for building my life. When I put God first, as the main character, I actually figured out who my character was. I saw more clearly the people in my life, not defined by what they've done to me or for me but by who God sees them as and by what He has done for them. And thus came my story of identity redemption. I went back to the moment I first truly believed and realized Jesus is the only reason our life matters in the end. But this time, God gave me the revelation that it's not just for eternal life, for the end, the individualized escapist theory, but for this life as well. I'm not living just to survive anymore.

IDENTITY REDEMPTION

In Joseph's story, God is the main character. So when we read that story, though we may connect and recognize ourselves in his character or with his brothers, we can't read it as a self-help book. He was not the main character, and neither are we. This is God's story. The Bible is not a self-help book. It is God's story and He is our helper. Hebrews 11 gives a long list of stories including Joseph's *"Great Examples of Faith."* But Hebrews 11:39–40 reads that *"all of these people we have mentioned received God's approval because of their faith, yet none of them received all that God had promised. For God had far better things in mind for us that would also benefit them, for they can't receive the prize at the end of the race until we finish the race."* In the Greek translation of this text, that last bit reads, *"For they, apart from us, can't finish."* So we are a part of Joseph's story as he is a part of our story. And through Christ, it is finished. He has made us one body with many parts. We have a purpose beyond our own individualized escapist theory. He is coming back again, and our purpose is to point to Him. And we can't point to Him if we don't know who He is, let alone where He is. When we come to know who He is, we should make Him the center point of our lives. This is not done by moving Jesus into the middle of our lives but by building our lives around Him.

One Sunday morning, a speaker at my church said that "there is nothing worse than a stale Christian." I thought, surely there is *something* worse. There are so many outright evil things in this world, and I thought, surely those are worse. But I understood his dramatic point that those things are so obviously not of God. But a stale Christian? A lukewarm Christian is confusing to others as to who God is. Our purpose is found in the Lord, and we are meant to point to Him and reflect Him. Our purpose is to reflect the Lord, but we are broken mirrors. A stale Christian says, "No, yeah, I follow God, but I also follow…" or "I'm a Christian, and I love all people just from afar" or "I love Jesus but the church, and I just don't get along," and that's not how this works. Imagine having a friend and saying, "He's great, but, *ugh*, his wife…" Being a lukewarm Christian is like being the friend that shows up for the parties but not for sicknesses or death.

I have always had this all-or-nothing mindset. And while in many things in life we can find a healthy balance, our faith is not one. No Christian is going to be the perfect Christian, but we must keep looking for and looking to God since we are a mirror; it is the only way to fulfill our purpose. It is either yes or no. Jesus said in Matthew 6:24 that *"no one can serve two masters. For you will hate one and love the other, or be devoted to one and despise the other."* I imagine the response, "Well, no, I don't hate God. Surely I don't hate God. I love God." And while I believe you, Judas also, in Matthew 26, said, surely it wouldn't be him who would betray Jesus, and surely it was. But Jesus died for Judas. Jesus loved Judas. We are not the main character, never have been and never will be. It's not about what we will or won't do. It's always been about Jesus, and it always will be. When we don't get this right, everything else is out of order. A stale Christian attempts to put Jesus at the center of their life, while a heart on fire for the Lord centers their life around Jesus.

CHAPTER 5

LOVE IS FORGIVING

God is a God of order, not disorder. He shares some of these orders in His word. His commandments are first to love Him then love others. But there's order in other things. He lays out some priorities and values for us to hold. He tells us love should be our highest goal. But what else does He give order to? He tells us that humility precedes honor, which makes sense, considering that love, although a thing of honor, is humble. We have to humble ourselves in order to receive His love. We can't be fully forgiven for sins if we won't admit we are a sinner. You can't save someone who doesn't think they need saving. I imagine throwing a life preserver at someone, and it's literally touching their arm, it's right there, and all they have to do is grab it, but they are convinced they don't need it, or maybe they are too busy holding on to other things that they won't let go of to grab what will save them. So they just keep treading water and fighting to stay afloat. They are prideful, even though they are drowning. Grace to someone who doesn't think they need it or forgiveness to someone who doesn't feel like they've done wrong still just feels like condemnation and disrespect. Have you ever tried to tell a narcissist that you have forgiven them? Telling them you forgive them is telling them they've done something wrong, something to require forgiveness, and they simply don't identify with that. But from humility comes honor.

> Haughtiness goes before destruction; humility precedes honor. (Proverbs 18:12)

In the Ten Commandments, it is written to *"honor your father and mother. Then you will live a long, full life in the land the Lord your God will give you"* (Exodus 20:12). I have a father who has misused this scripture. Sure, there were times as a child I was disrespectful, dishonoring, but those weren't really the times this scripture was recited to me. These scriptures were recited to me if I questioned my dad, disagreed with my dad, or told anyone something my dad did that didn't honor his reputation, even if they were true events. Growing up, honoring my father meant either he was perfect, or I was dishonoring. It meant that I was guilty, or he was guilty. Grace and forgiveness were rarely discussed in my home, unless of course as a condition to get someone to do something. It was flesh versus flesh. And being quite the fiery middle child yet oldest daughter that I was, I matched my dad's pride and responded to his use of scripture with Ephesians 6:1–4. Verses 1 through 3 read, *"Children, obey your parents because you belong to the Lord, for this is the right thing to do. 'Honor your father and mother.' This is the first of the Ten Commandments that ends with a promise: If you honor your father and mother, 'you will live a long life, full of blessing.'"* So with this, I said, "Yeah, you're right, Dad, but verse 4 reads, *'And now a word to you, fathers. Don't make your children angry by the way you treat them. Rather, bring them up with discipline and instruction approved by the Lord.'"* I shoved this in his face.

I often interjected myself into my mom and dad's screaming matches when my dad would use Scripture. I would find the

Scripture to combat what he had said. Looking back, I never really asked God what to do in those situations and responded based on my own understanding of Scripture. I was caught up in the flesh versus flesh as well. I was more concerned about being right than being righteous. Rightness is about approval and gratification through good works through yourself. Righteousness, though, is seeking to please God rather than yourself. It is recognizing that you are accepted based on what Jesus has done. We were both trying to be right, but we were both just being self-righteous and using God's word incorrectly. None of it was honoring to God.

In the Bible, discipline refers to training. Hebrews 12:10 reads, *"For our earthly fathers disciplined us for a few years, doing the best they knew how. But God's discipline is always right and good for us because it means we will share in his holiness."* My dad was not God; he didn't always get it right. But I can honor him by giving him grace. Humility precedes honor. God's word says the right thing to do is honor our parents. It doesn't say honor your parents if they do the right thing. I don't have to hold verse 4 over his head, like he held verses 1, 2, and 3 over mine. He did the best he knew how, but he isn't God. After talking to people older than me, I've decided that not only do I forgive him, but I count it forgotten, like Jesus does for me.

> And I will forgive their wrong doings, and
> I will never again remember their sins. (Hebrews 8:12)

My forgiveness is not forgiveness *if* he won't do it again or *because*. I don't honor my parents *if* I think they deserve it or *because*. True love is love *regardless*. Because the calling on my life is to love God with all my heart, all my soul, and all my mind, and because if I love him, I will obey Him, I can honor my parents simply because God said to. I can forgive simply because God said to. If God, the ultimate judge, has forgiven, then I will too. We love because He first loved us, and we can forgive because He first forgave us. When Christ is the foundation, we can build our responses to others based on His love. The love and forgiveness we can source is limited and often conditional, but from God it is unlimited and unconditional. And since He will honor us, we will honor others. Humility precedes honor.

When we humble ourselves to choose love, there is no record of wrongs. It's not just that there's no payback or penalty, but there's no record. So who did what, who said what doesn't matter. I used to think that Joseph's story, that when he chose love and chose to care for his brothers, that there was no justice. I was like, "What, his brothers don't have to really own up to their mistakes?" That is because the ending of the story wasn't there yet. It points to Jesus. The Bible is God's story. Our entire existence is part of God's story. The whole universe is His creation. And in Joseph's story, the veil wasn't torn yet. Jesus would take all the sin, all the blame, and bear all the shame to pay the price in full for Joseph's brothers, for me, for those who have wronged me, for you, and for those who have wronged you. Then when He rose from the grave three days later, He defeated it. So the blame is gone. The shame is gone. The price has been paid, and it has been paid in full. We cannot afford the price of our own wrongs, so who are we to demand others pay for what they've done to us? There is freedom in Christ. He paid for our forgiveness and for our salvation. What a love.

The main character of the story is Jesus. It's not about flesh and blood, who's good, who's bad, who's wrong, who's right, but it's the ultimate love story of redemption. We get to participate, and we already know who wins out. We don't get to choose who deserves or doesn't deserve this forgiveness or this grace or this love because we don't even deserve it. When we understand that God is the judge, we understand we are not. This means comparing the magnitudes of who did what is often a waste of time. Sin is sin. It separates us from God, no matter how small. God wants to be with *each* of His children, not just the ones we like. The price is paid for your sin and for those who have sinned against you. They are offered the same grace, love, and forgiveness as you, and we should rejoice if they choose to accept it. If we do not rejoice when those who have hurt us receive grace, forgiveness, and love, I can imagine the enemy rejoicing, knowing he's dividing families, robbing us of joy, and disrupting our healing.

> For we are not fighting against people made of flesh and blood, but against the evil rulers and authorities of the unseen world, against those mighty powers of darkness who rule this world, and against wicked spirits in the heavenly realm. (Ephesians 6:12)

When I think of forgiveness, I can't help but think of Cornelia "Corrie" ten Boom's story. Her story makes me feel miniscule and a bit pathetic that I have ever withheld forgiveness and had to spend months in therapy to forgive my father, myself, and others. What I learned though, is that I was trying to forgive from my own heart and efforts, not from the foundation of God's love. I was trying to forgive without being filled by God's heart. I heard her story, very briefly, in middle school, and I have not forgotten it. She was filled with God's heart.

If you aren't familiar, Corrie was a Dutch watchmaker and later a Christian writer and speaker. She, with her family, harbored hundreds of Jews during the Nazi Holocaust and was arrested. She was arrested and survived the horrors of concentration camp. In her freedom, she began traveling and telling people her story, preaching that God forgave sins and telling everyone that people needed to forgive those who've harmed them.

In 1947, she was speaking at a church and was greeted by a man after her speech. This man was one of the most vicious guards at the camp, and she recognized him. She wrote, from the moment of seeing him, *"It came back with a rush, the huge room with its harsh overhead lights; the pathetic pile of dresses and shoes in the center of the floor; the shame of walking naked past this man."* While she was experiencing the rush of memories, he put his hand out to shake hers and said how good it was to know that all their sins were at the bottom of the sea. He said he was one of the guards at the camp she had mentioned in her story and had since become a Christian, knowing God forgave him. But he wanted to hear from her that she forgave him as well. I cannot even imagine a fraction of Corrie's thoughts and emotions in this moment.

Corrie wrote that she *"wrestled with the most difficult thing I had ever to do. For I had to do it—I knew that. The message that God forgives has a prior condition: that we forgive those who have injured us."* So, *"Jesus, help me!"* She prayed. *"I can lift my hand. I can do that much. You supply the feeling."* And so, Corrie put her hand out. What she said and did next, I will never forget. To the Nazi guard of a women's concentration camp, the concentration camp she survived, she cried, *"I forgive you, brother! With all my heart."* She writes that *"for a long moment, we grasped each other's hands, the former guard and the former prisoner. I had never known God's love so intensely as I did then. But even so, I realized it was not my love. I had tried and did not have the power. It was the power of the Holy Spirit."*

I have no words to express my awe of God's forgiveness in this story. I remember thinking when I first heard it that if she can forgive him, I can forgive anyone. Evidently, I tried and did not have the power. Corrie called her former abuser, former prison guard, and former terrorist brother. She counted him as family. This is the power of God's love. The blood of Christ makes us family. It covers a multitude of sins. So for me to be counted as family is not by my own worth but through Christ. When I choose to accept this, I don't get to choose for anyone else to be in or out. It's not about me. Corrie knew that better than anyone. She was humble, faithful, and obedient to put her hand out and surrender to God.

The opposite of humility is pride. Our culture is prideful. We rejoice in being right but not in righteousness. We are lovers of ourselves and even have parades for pride in who we are. But there is much to say from Scripture about this. Jesus Himself said that *"it is the thought life that defiles you. For from within, out of a person's heart, come evil thoughts, sexual immorality, theft, murder, adultery, greed, wickedness, deceit, eagerness for lustful pleasure, envy, slander, pride, and foolishness. All these vile things come from within; they are what defile you and make you unacceptable to God"* (Mark 6:20–23). "It is the thought life that defiles you…" What is the thought life? Our sin begins in our minds. God knows every hair on our head and every thought in our head. He cares even for our thoughts and what we choose to think about. I imagine my thoughts spinning like The Price Is Right wheel. And when it stops on a thought or a thought comes to the front of my mind, I get to choose to spin again or think *about* that thought. I don't necessarily get to choose all the thoughts on the wheel, but I can choose to spin again.

Pride begins in our thoughts and specifically in our thoughts about our identity. Psychology research says that low self-esteem and self-worth are often the root causes of pride. I find that so interesting because pride is defined as confidence and satisfaction in oneself, having a high opinion of one's self and their own importance, deep pleasure from one's achievements, and consciousness of one's dignity. How then is the opposite of pride the root cause of pride?

Fear of vulnerability and a lack of self-accountability can lead to pride. So one may strive to combat low self-esteem, self-worth, and confidence with all they can achieve, trying to make themselves important, and searching for honor and respect to raise their dignity. I did. But honor is second to humility. We can't get second things by putting them first. The Bible tells us that *"pride leads to disgrace, but with humility comes wisdom"* (Proverbs 11:2) So by putting honor before humility, we actually get quite the opposite; we get disgrace. But by putting humility first, we get wisdom. Proverbs 14:1, one of my favorite Bible verses, says, *"A wise woman builds her house; a foolish woman tears hers down with her own hands."* So if with humility comes wisdom, I could read this verse to mean that a humble woman builds her house, but a prideful woman tears hers down. So to humble ourselves, we have to rewire our brain a little bit.

Our culture is prideful. But Romans 12:2 says, *"Don't copy the behavior and customs of this world, but let God transform you into a new person by changing the way you think. Then you will know what God wants you to do, and you will know how good and pleasing and perfect his will really is."* We are called to love with all our heart, all our soul, all our *mind*, and all our strength. We are called to give it our all. When Corrie surrendered to God by extending her hand, she then said she forgave him with all her heart. She loved God with all her heart. He filled her heart with a love that was not her own. So often we withhold our hand, we withhold the surrender, and so we don't love with *all* our heart or *all* our mind. We lean on our own understanding, which would never forgive a Nazi guard.

So to prioritize love, we what? First, we receive, then we make it practical. In our minds, to receive love, we have to accept that we can't earn it and don't deserve it. We have to humble ourselves. Then to make it practical, we have to surrender our minds. We have to extend our hand, and we should ask, "God, what do *You* want me to think about?" Don't worry too much about controlling your thoughts and surrendering your thoughts.

> Don't worry about anything; instead, pray about everything. Tell God what you need, and thank him for all he has done. If you do this, you will experience God's peace, which is far more wonderful than the human mind can understand. His peace will guard your hearts and minds as you live in Christ Jesus. And now, dear brothers and sisters, let me say one more thing as I close this letter. Fix your thoughts on what is true and honorable and right. Think about things that are pure and lovely and admirable. Think about things that are excellent and worthy of praise. (Philippians 4:6–8)

When the price is right, scroll of thoughts is going and going and stops. You surrender your mind to God by choosing to "spin again" if the thought is not honorable, right, pure, lovely, admirable, excellent, and worthy of praise. God will give you wisdom to discern these things if you ask for it. Asking for wisdom is humble because it is a proclamation that wisdom comes from God, not from our own understanding.

> For the Lord grants wisdom! (Proverbs 2:6)

> Trust in the Lord with all your heart; do not depend on your own understanding. (Proverbs 3:5)

Love loves justice. I didn't think Joseph's story was one of justice. But his brothers could have spent the rest of their lives paying for what they did and likely couldn't have afforded it. The Nazi guard certainly could have never made it up to Corrie. And when would enough be enough for who I see in the mirror or for a relationship with my dad? Justice comes from Jesus, who paid the price in full. So in forgiveness, there is justice. The love that counts our sins as forgotten is our justice. This is a humble justice. Jesus rights all our wrongs so when we walk with Jesus, we should find ourselves more concerned with righteousness rather than rightness because humility precedes honor.

CHAPTER 6

SWORD FIGHTS

A great way to spend time with God, come to recognize His voice, and renew our minds is by spending time reading and studying the word of God. The Bible is a gift from the Lord. God gives us His word to live on. The word of God reveals His character. It tells us who we are, what we should do, and it can comfort us. God moves in many ways far past any of our knowledge and comprehension, but one of those ways is in His word. Christ is referred to as the eternal Word. John 1:1–5 reads that *"in the beginning, the Word already existed. He was with God, and he was God. He was in the beginning with God. He created everything there is. Nothing exists that he didn't make. Life itself was in him, and this life gives light to everyone. The light shines through the darkness, and the darkness can never extinguish it."* So not only is Christ the center of our lives to build on, but He is the word of God. So the whole Bible is about Him. God is always true to His word. The word of God is alive and active. It is powerful.

> For the word of God is full of living power. It is sharper than the sharpest knife, cutting deep into our innermost thoughts and desires. It exposes us for what we really are. Nothing in all creation can hide from him. Everything is naked and exposed before his eyes. This is the God to whom we must explain all that we have done. (Hebrews 4:12)

God's word is our weapon. Satan loves to tell us lies and confuse us. God gives us His word so we will not be unprepared for that way to happen. We are told to stand firm in the armor of God to resist the enemy in order to stand firm. We are told to wear the belt of truth and wear the shoes of peace. We are told that we will need faith as our shield in every battle. Salvation is our helmet, and then our weapon is a sword. He says to *"take the sword of the Spirit, which is the word of God"* (Ephesians 6:17). Jesus used God's word to fight back against Satan. In Matthew 4, Jesus was led out into the wilderness and was tempted by the devil. He went hungry for forty days and forty nights. The devil came to Him and said that if He was the Son of God, then change the stones into loaves of bread. What Jesus did here is important. He didn't try to prove Himself to Satan. He didn't do what He was capable of and turn the stones into bread. Although he was hungry, he referenced the word of God and told Satan that *"the Scriptures say, 'People need more than bread for their life; they must feed on every word of God'"* (Matthew 4:4).

Satan took Him then to the highest point of the temple in Jerusalem and said, "Well, if you are the Son of God, jump off, because the Scriptures say that angels will protect you." So Satan also knows the word of God, making it even more important for us to study it. The word of God can be used for evil. Satan has twisted the words of God since the beginning of time. I've misused it, and I've had it misused against me. But Jesus responded to him, saying that *"the Scriptures also say, 'Do not test the Lord your God'"* (Matthew 4:7).

So Satan tried a third time, taking Jesus to the peak of a mountain and showing Him the nations of the world, telling Him to kneel down and worship him, and he'd give Him all of it. Satan was at his wit's end. Jesus told him to get out of there and told him, *"the Scriptures say, 'You must worship the Lord your God; serve only him'"* (Matthew 4:10). Jesus was confident in the Word and didn't waiver when it was used against Him. He obeyed the word of God. Jesus used the word of God to order Satan away and to defend Himself. We have this same power, not because of who we are but because the word of God is powerful. He could have proven Himself, turned the stone to bread, jumped off the temple, or told Satan off about the power of the nations of the world, but He didn't. He used the sword of the Spirit, the word of God. He is our example.

We are to know His word and know how to use it. The sword of the Spirit is not to be abused, like how Satan used it to try to control and manipulate Jesus's behavior. Satan, at first, wasn't telling Jesus to do anything necessarily wrong. He didn't tell Him to bow down to him right out of the gate. He simply asked Him to turn some bread to stone, something that would have proven who He was, proven God's power, and satisfied His hunger. But Satan is tricky like this. Like I said, he loves to lie to us and confuse us. He didn't directly ask Jesus to bow down to him at first, but each request was leading there. Jesus didn't act based on Satan's requests or actions but on the word of God and used the sword of the Spirit. Who Jesus was did not change just because Satan was trying to make Him doubt it. For a God that loves justice and loves when the truth wins out, He doesn't seem to ever retaliate in defense of Himself. As someone who felt, for a long time, like I was constantly on defense, using the word of God the way my dad did—this is interesting to me.

We see in Scripture that Jesus often presented an apologetic, a defense of doctrine and principle, but not often a defense in the way we would think, like turning the stone to bread or jumping, instead he's known for turning the other cheek. Why is that? When Jesus was with Simon Peter, in Matthew 26 and in Mark 14, Simon Peter cut the ear off a guard as they grabbed Jesus and arrested Him. Jesus's response to this explains to me why he was never too concerned about what the enemy was asking of him or accusing him of. He had a confidence in something greater than the moment and greater than his feelings.

> "Put away your sword," Jesus told him. "Those who use the sword will be killed by the sword. Don't you realize that I could ask my Father for thousands of angels to protect us, and he would send them instantly? But if I did, how would the Scriptures be fulfilled that describe what must happen now?" Then Jesus said to the crowd, "Am I some dangerous criminal that you have come armed with swords and clubs to arrest me? Why didn't you arrest me in the Temple? I was there teaching every day. But this is all happening to fulfill the words of the prophets as recorded in the Scriptures." (Matthew 26:52–56)

Jesus did not come to build a kingdom like that of Alexander or Genghis Khan. He knew Scripture, He knew the Father, and He knew a greater kingdom coming, a bigger story than that of His arrest. Though in the moment, He was given the title of a criminal, He still had the identity of a King. He knew He was the Son of God. He knew His purpose. He was an example for us in moments like this of our purpose. We are called to love *first*. We are called to reflect the Lord, not to retaliate. Retaliation is a reflection of circumstances; it's a grasping for power. Jesus was never grasping for power. In moments He looked weak to the crowd, not using the swords of the world, He had more courage and strength than most men will ever know, using the sword of the Spirit. It takes courage to love rather than retaliate. Movements have been inspired by this courage, by this example for our purpose.

Take Martin Luther King Jr. for example. He did not lead a violent revolt against injustice, which might have proven his point but would have defeated his purpose. Or we can even take a look at the similarity in Gandhi's aims. This was all Jesus inspired.

The purpose of the word of God is not to prove our points. The Bible is human history through the lens of Israel. Moreover, the Bible is God's story; it is about Jesus. The Bible tells us first who He is, then who we are, and what our purpose is. When we use Scripture to solely prove a point, like Satan did to Jesus, we have gotten the characters out of order. We have made ourselves the main character. Like I said before, when we regard ourselves as the main character, we put God's entire purpose for us out of focus. We are called to live for a purpose, not to prove a point.

The Bible is a gift from God and is a great way to spend time with God, come to recognize His voice, and renew our minds. Getting to know the word of God is a great way to get to know God. Through studying Scripture, I've come to recognize moves of God in my own life and God's voice. I've gained confidence in knowing who I am because I am His. He has revealed Himself to me in sweet, sweet ways through encounters I've recognized by knowing the word of God. He has given me a story of identity redemption, not just for who I am but for who He is and who others in my life are through His eyes. The defense of our identity is not a matter of flesh versus flesh. Jesus had Simon Peter put his sword down for, I believe, this very purpose. The word of God stands true. Jesus has already overcome.

What God says is final. So when God said Joseph would be in a position of leadership over his brothers, no worldly transaction, enslavement, accusation, or prison could change the outcome. What's prevalent then is our faith. Will we have faith in the sword of the Spirit or reach for something more tangible to our flesh, the swords of this world? God is who He says He is, and we are who He says we are.

> Your word is a lamp to my feet and a light for my path. (Psalm 119:105)

CHAPTER 7

GOD, *WHO* ARE YOU?

Our identity is based on our relationship with God. In chapter 1, I said that I knew God as a Savior, but I found *my identity* when I began to know Him as a friend, as a Father, a provider, a comforter, a healer, a protector, my strength, my endurance, and my Lord. Because knowing Him as a friend, a Father, a provider, comforter, healer, a protector, my strength, my endurance, and my Lord means I am a daughter of the King, a friend of Jesus, cared for, loved, cherished, protected, safe, strong, and that I can endure tests, trials, tribulations, and temptations. Our identity is found in relationship with God. The definition of a relationship is the state of being connected. Our identities are connected to who God is. So perhaps the question we should ask is not "God, where were you?" but rather "God, who are you?"

When I say that I knew God as a Savior, it means that I was the main character in my individualized escapist theory. I separated

Savior from Lord of my life. But I want to share with you some of the ways I've come to know God and a few of the ways He has revealed Himself as these things in the Bible. Who we truly are is found in relationship with who God is.

The world defines us by our accomplishments and performances, our reputations, and our appearances. The world gives us labels—some hurtful, some helpful, but none as true as what God calls us. God is our Creator. Our minds, abilities, and personalities were created by His design. Nothing about you is a mistake to be fixed. God took a look at the world He created, His plan, and placed you in the family He wanted you in, in the country, the city, or the town He wanted you in for a reason.

When I was a child, crying, "Why me, God?" God spent many years showing me exactly why. I grew up, and one question I learned not to ask was "why?" The answer would always be because I told you so. Oftentimes, our parents have good reasons for what they tell us to do, even if we don't understand. The cool thing about God is that when you ask him why, when you don't understand or are maybe even scared, He not only allows our questions but desires them. Whether or not He reveals why or when He reveals why, I can't tell you. But I can tell you, He is trustworthy and has a plan for all of our lives. Because He has a plan, there is a purpose for each of us in it. Faith is trusting God before He tells us why. We want to know why and lean on our own understanding and decide if it makes sense to us or if we agree before we walk. Walking by faith often disregards our own understanding and asks us to lean on the Lord. The Bible tells us that faith "*is the confident assurance that what we hope for is going to happen. It is the evidence of things we cannot yet see*" (Hebrews 11:1).

When God asks us to have faith, He isn't telling us we can't have doubts. But Jesus said, *"Even if you had faith as small as a mustard seed you could say to this mountain, 'Move from here to there,' and it would move. Nothing would be impossible"* (Matthew 17:20). So Jesus said, with even a mustard seed of faith, nothing would be impossible. God only asks us to muster up enough faith to equate to a mustard seed. In our barely hanging on "why God?" seasons, we just need a mustard seed of faith. In Matthew 9, there was a woman who had a hemorrhage and was bleeding for twelve years. She came up behind Jesus and touched the fringe of His robe, and Matthew 9:21 says, *"For she thought, 'If I can just touch his robe, I will be healed.'"* Something God asked me to do a long time ago is to "doubt my doubt." If I can so easily doubt God, would I just put my energy into doubting my doubt *first*? I encourage you to doubt your doubt enough to be like the woman who reached out to touch His robe. Just reach out for the Lord. He's waiting for you, and He has healing for you.

I encourage you and pray for you to have the faith to trust that God is who He says He is in His word and expect Him to show up as such. Any relationship we have requires trust, and who we are has everything to do with who He is. Without Him, it's no wonder we find ourselves lost. The God of the Old Testament, of the beginning of time, is the same God of today. Look for Him. Welcome Him. It might feel inconvenient, but it is important. Welcome interruption from the Lord. When you disregard your divine appointments as disruptions, you risk missing what God might have to tell you or show you. Remember that being followers of Christ, being Christians, is not so much about inviting Him into our story as much as it is about yielding to His, for which we were created. This is His story, and you are wanted in it. You are loved. You were created for it. Your life is not your own. We are followers before we are leaders. He is leading us. He is the Lord of all.

God is the Creator. He created everything. He created man, and He created woman. But when sin separated us from Him, He was not worried, for He had a plan as our Father for our family. He created us to know Him and to be with Him in relationship, not just religion. Even when we haven't loved Him, He has loved us and continues to love us. So He sent His one and only Son, Jesus, to die for us on the cross. The cost of sin is death, and He paid the price for all our sins, took the blame though blameless, and died. He rose three days later and ascended to heaven, promising to return again for His people. He closed the gap, and He defeated the separation between us and God. He was the ultimate sacrifice. So then God is our Father, not just by creation but by conception.

When you receive the love of Christ demonstrated through the crucifixion and resurrection, you are made new. You are born again into the family of God.

> Jesus replied, "I assure you, unless you are born again, you can never see the Kingdom of God." "What do you mean?" exclaimed Nicodemus. How can an old man go back into his mother's womb and be born again?" Jesus replied, "The truth is, no one can enter the Kingdom of God without being born of water and the Spirit. Humans can reproduce only human life, but the Holy Spirit gives new life from heaven. So don't be surprised at my statement that you must be born again.'" (John 3:3–7)

When you are born again with new life from heaven from the Holy Spirit, God is your Father, and you are a daughter or a son of God.

> And I will be your Father, and you will be my sons and daughters, says the Lord Almighty. (2 Corinthians 6:18)

God is the Creator of all. Christ is the Lord of all. But God is only the Father of those born into His family. By being born into His family, you are made new and are given an identity as a daughter or son of God the King. You are royalty, in a way, through even a mustard seed of faith in this. Before Jesus, people were saved by their faith, for they did not know what was coming but had faith far greater than a mustard seed. Our faith makes us family.

God the Father is also our protector. There is a song you may know called "Surrounded" by Upperroom. The beginning of the song says, "There's a table that you've prepared for me in the presence of my enemies," which alludes to Psalm 23. God *blesses* us in the presence of our enemies. He keeps us and protects us in their

IDENTITY REDEMPTION

presence. He sits us before them because He is with us. God is for us. And since He is for us, nothing can be against us (Romans 8:31). He is our protector. Receiving His blessings takes faith because while He is our shield, we can see the offense. We can see the weapons formed against us but have to trust that they won't prosper because He is our defense. He is also our strength.

> I love you, Lord; you are my strength. The Lord is my rock, in whom I find protection. He is my shield, the strength of my salvation, and my stronghold. (Psalm 18:1–2)

I said in chapter 4 that I prided myself on being strong, but God wanted to use my weaknesses. God is our strength. In 2 Corinthians 12, Paul had a thorn in his flesh that kept him from getting puffed up or prideful. He said, *"Three different times I begged the Lord to take it away. Each time he said 'my gracious favor is all you need. My power works best in your weakness.' So now I am glad to boast about my weaknesses, so that that power of Christ may work through me. Since I know it is all for Christ's good, I am quite content with my weaknesses and with insults, hardships, persecutions, and calamities. For when I am weak, then I am strong"* (2 Corinthians 12:8–10).

For so long I was told to have shame disguised as strength. I was told not to talk about having PANS/PANDAS. I was threatened that the world would be shown who I really was through videos of me having an episode. I was told not to talk about my dad because who would they believe? I was told not to tell my story because to tell my story would mean to highlight my weaknesses. I was told to hide. But God tells something different. He tells us to boast about our weakness because the power of Christ works best in our weakness. God knows we will deal with insults, hardships, persecutions, and calamities, like Paul. But not only is He our strength, He is our comfort and our endurance. Because we are His sons and daughters, He treats us as such and teaches us endurance through discipline. He gives us hope, a promise to remember that *"as you endure this divine discipline, remember that God is treating you as his own children"*

(Hebrews 12:7). God's discipline for us is not like our earthly fathers; it is always right and good for us. Jesus said, *"Those who endure to the end will be saved"* (Matthew 24:13). Endurance is a gift from God; pain is just the packaging. We don't have to puff ourselves up with pride in the midst of pain to protect ourselves. There is no shame in the presence of God. He wants our weakness. He already knows our weakness.

In our pain though, he is our comforter.

> God offers comfort to all. All praise to the God and Father of our Lord Jesus Christ. He is the source of every mercy and the God who comforts us. He comforts us in all our troubles so that we can comfort others. While others are troubled, we will be able to give from the same comfort God has given us. You can be sure that the more we suffer for Christ, the more God will shower us with his comfort through Christ. So when we are weighed down with troubles, it is for your benefit and salvation! For when God comforts us, it is so that we, in turn, can be an encouragement to you. Then you can patiently endure the same things we suffer. We are confident that as you share in suffering, you will also share in God's comfort. (2 Corinthians 1:3–7)

So once again, it's just not really about us. We are not the main character. It is all for the Lord. He is our Father, our protector, our strength, our endurance, and our comforter. He is many things including our peace and our provider. But He is also our friend. So not only are we family, but Christ has declared us friends. How much of your family are you friends with?

Jesus demonstrated this in John 15:15–16 after He commands us to love each other in the same way He loves us. He said to His disciples, *"I no longer call you servants, because a master doesn't confide in his servants. Now you are my friends, since I have told you everything the*

Father told me. You didn't choose me. I chose you." Jesus calls us friends because He tells us what the Father tells Him. We have a friend in Jesus, a Father in God, and a family with our new life in the Holy Spirit. I included the beginning of verse 16 because not only does Jesus call us friends, but He makes it clear that He chose us, not the other way around. What does that say about our identity?

CHAPTER 8

THE PROPOSAL WITHOUT A RING

We are made in the image of God, and we are made for relationships with Him. Our relationship with Him has a direct correlation to our identity. But when we don't have what we were created for—a relationship with the Lord—something will always be missing, something we can't find in a self-help book or any other relationship. Trust me, I've tried to find it elsewhere. Without Christ as the center and foundation, our identity will always be misplaced. When Jesus calls us friends, He makes it clear that He has chosen us, not the other way around. We are chosen, no matter what! He is kind to the unthankful. We don't determine who God is, but He does tell us who we are. He has a calling on each of our lives. Whether we choose to fulfill our calling is our choice though.

When we choose to be followers and disciples of Christ, we choose to be the church. We become His bride. The Word tells us the church is Jesus's bride. For some, I know that can be hard, because the church is full of people, which means sin, which means hurt, and which means brokenness. But we have to remember this is about Jesus, so what might mean sin, hurt, and brokenness, also means forgiveness, family, and healing. As Paul described in Ephesians 4:4–6, *"We are all one body, we have the same Spirit, and we have all been called to the same glorious future. There is only one Lord, one faith, one baptism, and there is only one Father who is over us all and in us all and living through us all,"*

We get to choose to say yes to God and come under His fatherhood and into His family. This offer doesn't expire, but I urge you to waste no time. Like you wouldn't want to waste time to join the love of your life found in a man, may you know the love of your life from the Lord. I see a proposal from the Lord. But instead of getting on one knee, He got on the cross for you. He gave His life for you. He forgives you, and He loves you. You get to become His bride or reject it. You can break His heart, but you can't change His mind about you. When we are in a relationship with God though, when we have said yes to Him, our identity has been redeemed. We gain an identity as friends of Jesus, as a daughter or a son of the King, protected, safe, provided for, and more. We get to leave behind the identity the world gives us, even our own friends and family. We get to leave behind the fear of what we could become and the expectation of what we think should become.

When we choose to receive the love from God, from the crucifixion and resurrection of our friend Jesus, we are born in the Holy Spirit and made new as daughters and sons of God, of the King. We are saved, forgiven. The slate is wiped clean. We are new, blameless in His eyes, and we are redeemed. God created us as such sons and daughters, and we've always been seen as such by Him. God created us for this relationship but doesn't force us into it. Sin separated us from God in the beginning with Adam and Eve. But the Lord made a way and is the way back to relationship to Him, back to our purpose and original identity. When Jesus came into the world, He came to save it, not condemn it. But like we know, offering salvation to someone who doesn't think they need it can feel pretty insulting and jabs at their pride and their egos. It did to mine. Pride says I don't need saving, while humility says thank you for saving me. Pride says I had it right, while humility says thank you for showing me the way. Pride is haughty and arrogant, while humility is unpretentious and grateful. We are in a world full of pride and egos, and we build our identities around them and around what we can accomplish. We like trophies on shelves that we can see now and show others, not trophies in heaven. Our identities are redeemed when we choose the Lord instead of the world. He has already overcome the world and invites us into victory with Him, to be in the world but not of the world.

He paid the price for our sins to make Himself available to us. He is literally the definition and standard for "if he wanted to, he would" ladies. This is a relationship you want and a proposal you should accept. If you can romanticize a guy with a mediocre mullet, you can ask for even just a mustard seed of faith for this relationship. It is worth it. He humbled Himself by being God Almighty and coming into the earth as man. If that's not humbling enough, He was born in a manger, which is like a trough, a feeder for animals. I think it's interesting how from the moment He was born, it pointed to Him feeding us as He is the bread of life. Through Him, we are fulfilled. He brings to fruition our purpose and identity. He lived a humble life as a carpenter until His time of public ministry around the age of thirty at the end of which He would be beaten on a cross that He carried for crimes He didn't commit. He did this in place of a man named Barabbas, a common criminal, who is symbolic for me and symbolic for you, common sinners. We are Barabbas. Three days later, He would be resurrected, though, and ascend to heaven, promising to return again for the second resurrection, the resurrection of His people, for Barabbas, for you and me. The bridegroom is coming back for His bride. While this might be the longest amount of time literally ever for someone to say yes or no to a proposal, I urge you to waste no time because the next second is not promised. We don't know when He will return, but He is coming.

The Bible has much to say about, first, who God is, then who we are and what our purpose is, and I urge you to spend time in the word of God to learn more and more about Him, about yourself, and about your individual purpose. Spending time in the word of God familiarizes you with His character and helps you to recognize Him and His voice in your own life to build that relationship with Him that redeems your identity. Ask Him to reveal Himself, and He will. He wants you to know Him. I can offer you truth after truth from my own little bit of time in the Word and my encounters, experiences, and divine appointments with the Lord, but there is a deep mystery of the Lord. You can meet with Him daily, spend your life studying, and there would still be so much we don't understand. But I understand these things: He is good, He is who He says He is, and there is a standing proposal for us. This is a proposal for you to not only be saved and have eternal life but to step into a relationship with God into your true identity and into His story.

The Word tells us that God is our Creator, our Father, our protector, our strength, our comforter, our endurance, and our friend. There is a list exponentially longer than this with each description of who God is, having a correlation to who we are. Knowing who God is and who we are allows us to discombobulate the lies of the enemy, as we'll know who He is NOT and who we are NOT. We have faith in the Lord and confidence in who He is, therefore we can stand firm and be confident in who we are, even if it's just a mustard seed of this faith. He redeems our identities with even a mustard seed of faith. Since God is my Creator, I am a creation, here on purpose, not an accident and not misplaced. I will doubt my doubt that I am something different. Since God is my Father, since I have been born again in the Spirit, I am a daughter of God, the King Most High. I belong to the Lord. I have a place in His family. Since God is my protector, I am not afraid. I am safe. He is for me, and nothing can stand against me. He is my strength, so in my weakness, because of Him, I am strong. The enemy has no foothold by highlighting my weaknesses, for I am content. The light has been shone already, and shame has no place here. He is my comforter and my endurance, meaning I find comfort in Him, and I will endure. I am a friend of Jesus. These are a great starting place for a foundation of who God is and who we are. Our identities are based on this, not on what we have or haven't done or what anyone else has said. We can declare these things confidently and know who we are because we are His. Our identity, when found in the Lord, is unwavering, steady, and fixed because the Lord is our rock—unwavering, steady, and fixed. He is constant, and He is consistent.

He is worthy of our worship for who He is. I can't say it enough that He is truly worthy. He is who He says He is. But I was convicted and found myself, for so long, worshipping the story of my pain and not my Redeemer for the story of my redemption. I was in the individualist-escapist theory version of Christianity. And instead of worshipping the Lord who had redeemed me, I was lukewarm, saved from my sin but still choosing to live in it. I was living to prove I was not the horrid things said about me or done to me. I was living to prove I wasn't a diagnosis or a label. I was living to prove I wasn't the picture the enemy showed and told me was a mirror. But proving a point is not the point of my existence. I'm not supposed to be looking in a mirror all my life but to be a mirror looking to God.

I used to say that the pain gave me purpose. If you ever saw my Instagram or my TikTok, it was clear for a while that I wasn't living for God, but I was living to spite my pain. Worship is not just about singing a song, but it is a heart posture and is a way of life. Worship is an offering of our deepest affections and highest praise, so what we center our lives on, what drives us, is what we're worshipping. I worshipped my pain for too long. I had a drive, and I was a hustler to prove these points. But the pain never gave me purpose. I *found* purpose in the pain. The Lord drew me to Himself and pursued me. I was lost, and now I'm found. I got in the Word and asked Him to reveal Himself to me, and He did. I was found in the midst of my pain. God met me in the midst of my pain and invited me to meet Him, to get to know Him. I had a purpose all along; I just found it in the pain because I was found in the pain. My purpose came from who found me because He also created me, and He redeemed me. My identity was redeemed. So I don't want to live to spite my pain because that was never the point of my pain. I want to live for God and, more importantly, to live *with* God as I was created to, to meet Him as He meets me, to wait expectantly for Him to show up because He does, and He will. My pain may be present, but my God has never been absent.

CHAPTER 9

THE FEELS

I want to worship Him who is truly worthy. I want to center my life on Him. I want to follow Him. He is worthy above all else. He is trustworthy above all else. I was raised to be very antifeelings. Feelings were often hurt in my home but not discussed. We rubbed some dirt on it, enough dirt to bury it, and moved on. The intentions were good. I had military parents who wanted to raise respectful, tough, resilient kiddos. For some reason, being emotionally healthy did not fit the description of respectful, tough, and resilient. Crying was not tough, but avoiding tough feelings somehow was. But inconveniently for their philosophy, they ended up with a child with PANS/PANDAS, who had no healthy example to deal with her feelings. I kept things in. This made me a "respectful, tough, resilient kiddo," but I was really just acting according to my learned knowledge that it was better to lie than to say what someone didn't want to hear, to never express feelings, to tiptoe around unpredictable changes in people's behavior, and not be affected by anything ever, or I was weak. It was better to hurt myself than to share my burdens with others. I internalized my feelings and took them on as part of my identity.

God had healing for me though. In high school, right before I started working five jobs and spiraling off the flight end of fight-or-flight, I was sexually assaulted. Shame weighed so heavy that I internalized my assault as having something to do with my identity. It eventually came out in an unhealthy way. But as I came out of survival mode, God had healing for me. God wanted my weakness. I didn't have to be strong.

I never would've thought I'd have centered my life on my feelings nor even worshipped my pain, considering I was living to avoid it. But by living to avoid my feelings, I lived around them. By trying to avoid my feelings, I actually centered my life on them, and they began to control me. The means through which I tried to control my life began to control me. Though I was taught that "nobody cares about the labor pains; they just want to see the baby," I felt like I couldn't make it through my labor pains to ever show a baby. Please know, this is just an analogy and has nothing to do with bearing a child.

I've learned, though, that God actually does care. He cares, really. I assumed we shouldn't care about our feelings, and I assumed God didn't care about our feelings, especially since He knows who has it far worse. I know that the world, in general, doesn't care about our feelings, unless it can be used for marketing, profit, or manipulation. But God took the time to make it known to me that He cares about my feelings. He cares about our labor pains, not just the baby. He has compassion. He is fully aware of our humanness and the things we feel. I don't believe he is angered at our humanness. He wants our weakness, for in it, Christ's power is perfect.

He addresses our humanness in the Bible through the story of Elijah in 1 Kings. Elijah had upset some prophets in Baal, and the evil queen Jezebel was ticked all the way off. Elijah fled for his life from her into the wilderness. In the wilderness, he sank into a depression and fell asleep, just exhausted. He was woken up by an angel who fed him, let him rest some more, eat some more, and gain enough strength to continue to safety in the mountains. Elijah was human and had limitations. God is aware of our limits and our humanness. He knows sometimes we will need a nap and a snack to do what He's asking us to do. He provides for us in our humanness. He meets us where we are. He wants us in our labor pains, whether we have a baby to show for it or not. He wants us, not our Trophy shelves. Whether implicitly or explicitly, we are often told, "You can't be human."

We are told to keep going and to overcome. Elijah pushed through until he fell asleep while fleeing for safety, just simply exhausted. He had prayed for God to take his life. Finding the strength to continue seemed so impossible to Elijah that he prayed that he might die. God says, "I know you're a human, but because you're mine, that doesn't define you." He meets us in our humanness. He is our strength, our endurance, and our provider. Angels are from the Lord, and His holy provision was a snack and a nap because He knows our needs. Whether it's a physical need or an emotional need, God is aware of our humanness. Elijah met God in the mountains at safety, and God didn't come to him as an earthquake, a shining light, or anything dramatic. He came in a gentle whisper. When we stop trying to deny our humanness, stop trying to be gods, avoid our depression, avoid our hunger, avoid our exhaustion, or avoid our feelings, we are able to encounter the Lord, who may come in a gentle whisper. He cares about every need, even the need for a nap and a snack. He cares about us in our humanness.

When I've looked back and asked God where He was during what felt like my "flees," I realized He was provided many "snacks and naps." I didn't always feel God, but God is not a feeling. I don't have this singular moment that God really made Himself known to me, but I do have a series of gentle whispers I heard when I didn't deny my humanness and have accepted God's proposal. Though I didn't *feel* Him at times in my story, when I listened, I heard the gentle whispers. When I looked back and asked God where He was in my story, I learned that God is not a feeling. God has many roles and works in many ways. Some of these we can feel; some we can't. If we only know God as a feeling, of course, we will mistake the absence of familiar feelings for the absence of God.

God cares for our feelings. However, feelings are to feel, not to follow. Jesus demonstrated this within a detail of the crucifixion. In Mark 14:24, Jesus said, *"I solemnly declare that I will not drink wine again until that day when I drink it new in the Kingdom of God."* In Mark 15:23, Jesus refused the wine drugged with myrrh offered to Him before He was about to endure unimaginable pain on our behalf. Wine and myrrh created an aesthetic herb that lessens pain. I don't doubt that Jesus knew this. He went through the crucifixion and cried out to God, *"Eloi, Eloi, lema sabachthani?"* which means, "My God, My God, why have You forsaken me?" They bring Him more sour wine in Mark 15:36. He didn't drink it. And in Mark 15:37, it says, *"Jesus uttered another loud cry and breathed his last."* This is not about wine. He kept His word despite His feelings. He chose to honor the truth over comfort and relief. His promise meant more to Him than His pain. He knew who He was, and He knew His purpose. He died a shameful death in honor. He did this for me, and He did this for you. He loves us, and He loves you relentlessly. His word is true and to be followed, unlike our feelings that are fleeting.

Jesus was a prime example that we are human. We will have pain and hunger and feelings of "Why, God, have You forsaken me?" We can feel our feelings, but we shouldn't follow them. We can be angry, but the Bible says not to sin in our anger. We can be sad or happy or depressed or anxious but must remember our feelings are not our identities nor our compass for decision-making. Feelings are not something to run from nor something to run with. A book I have loved reading called *Why Has Nobody Told Me This Before?* by Dr. Julie Smith, a clinical psychologist, touches on this topic as well. She wrote that *"each emotion, behavior, and period in our lives is temporary and not necessarily a reflection of who we are permanently... It's much harder to change an identity as an anxious person than it is to simply reduce anxiety."* We are not what we feel; we are who God says we are.

But I can't deny my humanness. Sometimes, like Elijah, I just collapse and have felt like I couldn't take it any longer. So one way I've learned to feel my feelings and not follow them is by understanding them more. I've done this through a lot of reflection and journaling and also some therapy and counseling. We don't have to fear our feelings or avoid our weaknesses. I can confidently approach them because God is with me, and my identity comes from Him. We are told to share each other's burdens as well. So by keeping in our pain, we are actually disobeying the Lord.

> Share each other's troubles and problems, and in this way obey the law of Christ. (Galatians 6:2)

Though we are in the world, we are not *of* the world when we belong to God. So what *feels* right may not be right. Our identity doesn't have much to do with what we *feel* like. There's no need or point in being prideful or in being ashamed of our feelings. I was prideful when I learned to hide how I felt, and I was prideful in my own strength and success. I was ashamed though when I felt dirty, out of control, broken, weak, and used. When we base our identities off of our feelings, our identities fluctuate as our feelings fluctuate, and we don't know who we are. Feelings are fleeting and provide insecure footing. God is not. He is constant and steady. It is no wonder that we find ourselves insecure finding our identity in our feelings or our ever-changing circumstances. You can know exactly who you are by knowing who God is. We can't really control our feelings, but it's what we do with them that we can control. When we surrender that control to God and get to know Him and be more and more like Him, I believe emotional health comes with that. He asks us to come to Him with all these things. He cares.

Though we may experience anxiety, we shouldn't identify as anxious. Though we may struggle with depression, our identity is not depressed. Our identity is not found in our feelings or our circumstances in the world. Joseph didn't always look like who God made him to be, and I bet he didn't always feel like who God made him to be. But despite his circumstances and despite his feelings, he was who God said he would be. When Jesus was taken away, I bet it didn't look like heaven was winning. When He was carrying His cross to Calvary, I bet it didn't feel like He was carrying a victory. I bet the beating He received didn't feel like the honor He was promised. And when He died, I bet the enemy felt victorious. But despite how everything looked and despite all these feelings, God's plan prevailed, and look who rose victorious. Victory belongs to the Lord.

We are in the world, not of the world. I thought for so long when I would give my feelings and my pain to God that He was disregarding my feelings with what He might tell me to do because it wasn't making me feel better. The problem wasn't God. I wasn't letting go of my feelings or my pain because I found identity in them. I didn't find identity in the victory to come but in what I felt like. Imagine if Joseph did this. Imagine if Jesus did this! This was a hard pill to swallow when I was convicted of this. When we give Him our feelings and ask Him what to do, we have to actually let go of our feelings. Imagine giving someone a gift but never letting go of the gift bag handles as they reach for it. Awkward. How often do we do that to God though? "Lord, here, take this from me, but don't expect me to let go of it." It's time to let go of who you've been, who you are, and who you think you might become, and it is time to lean into the identity God gives you.

CHAPTER 10

PEACE

If you live in America, you have probably heard to "let go and let God" more times than you can count but have also likely heard the screams of hustle culture to have a vision and a goal at all times. Hustle culture says we are lost without them, but more often we get lost in the hustle. Hustle culture and Christianity cross paths often. They did on my podcast in almost every episode. When we say we are lost without our own vision and goals, that's another way of saying, "I'm living by my own will and leaning on my understanding." We want to be good stewards and good managers of the resources we have but must be careful to not try to be the boss. We must remember to ask the Lord for wisdom and not lean on our own understanding. In my podcast, I talked about how confidence comes from doing what you said you would do. That is self-confidence. We shouldn't be placing our confidence in ourselves though but in God. We should be less worried about saying what we'll do and more on listening for what God says to do. I quoted on the podcast something I read while scrolling Instagram that "worry looks around. Fear looks back, and faith looks forward." What we look to shows where we have placed our faith. If we are looking to God, then our faith is in God. If we are looking to our own plans and goals, then our faith is in ourselves and our hustle. If we are looking at what people around us are doing or the people that we want to be like, that's where our faith is. I don't want faith in myself, in the hustle, or in the world. I have faith in the Lord. I hyped up the idea of making vision boards and did so for a couple years. I would ask myself daily what I did that day to get to each of the goals I had pasted on this board. This board was to visualize what I was pursuing. But how often did I ask God what He wanted or had planned for my life? I was looking at these vision boards every day, and it wasn't until I started looking to God every day that my identity was redeemed.

Most books for young adults are going to tell you how to set up your life, how to kick-start your career, give relationship and dating advice, financial advice, and all the self-help topics I used to be so focused on. These are great as second things. The most important thing I want you to know is not a thing but a who. If you do nothing else, get to know the Lord. After reading this book, I hope, if you learned anything, you learned to look for God. He's waiting for you. I see a picture of a greeter or driver at an airport with a sign, waiting. You may not know what they look like, but you know to look for your name on the sign. God has a sign with your name on it, and He is waiting for you, looking for you, and will never give up on you. He may redeem your identity, He may redeem a whole nation through you, He may heal you, or He may heal others through you—I don't know. But what I do know is that He has a plan, the perfect plan, and that His plans always prevail.

> You can make many plans, but the Lord's
> purpose will prevail. (Proverbs 19:21)

I am finishing writing this book just a few days after my twentieth birthday in November of 2023. I tend to be more reflective on birthdays, looking back at the past year, prayers I may have written for the age I just ended, etc. Last November, I prayed that in my Bible reading, I would get to know God more and who He says I am more. Needless to say, He answered this prayer, and He continues to answer this prayer of mine in ways I never imagined when I prayed it. In February of this year, I prayed over the start of this book. I said, "If I wrote a book" and then I said, "When I write a book." I asked what it should be about, what the message would be, what the story would be, and who it was for. I asked God to help me answer these questions and to help me be honest and honor Him. I prayed that this book would speak truth and life and that people would be better for having read it. I prayed that it would bring light and make people laugh and was sure to specify that it would make people laugh but not at it. I wrote down a brief idea for what each chapter of the book would be about, and it was all the things I mentioned that most young adults are already served for self-improvement. It was the book version of my podcast, where I got a lot wrong and, more so, a lot out of order. The topic of God and faith was a chapter, a part of the story. But the reality is that this is God's story, and we are a part of it, not the other way around.

I feel more fear in finishing this book than I did in quitting my job to write this book. I think that is because I don't know what's next. I don't have a goal or a solid plan to be honest. I just know that my eyes are fixed on God. I know who I am, no matter what comes. I have peace, and I have joy, and I have confidence, though I have no clue what's next. The world says I need a clear vision and a goal to avoid failure. My own flesh says that too. But I know my identity is not one of a failure but a follower. I don't know what's next. I don't know where I'm going. I just know that obedience to God is my responsibility, and the outcome it brings is not. I have peace in this because God is peace.

I have a journal with my one- to two-year goals, my three- to four-year goals, my five- to six-, my seven- to eight-, my nine- to ten-, and my constant/daily life goals. These are the goals that were on the vision boards. Finishing this book marks just over a year from when I made this list of goals, which was exactly two weeks after I started the job I quit to write this book. I've said before that I don't set goals; I write to do lists. But now, love is my highest goal. Knowing the Lord is the priority, so my to-do is to listen and obey for all the days of my life. Through writing this book, I've realized I didn't quit my job to write this book but to surrender my life to God. He is my focus, and I've been brought back to the moment I first truly knew Him, not just of Him and not just the individualized escapist theory. He brought me back to the moment I first knew Him and began a relationship with Him that I've told you bits about in this book. He showed me who He is, was, and will always be and who I am and was created to be. I trust Him, I love Him, and I am so thankful.

This is not to say that having goals is a bad thing, but if we say God first, He must come before all of them. You don't get second things by putting them first, and all is second to the Lord. What God has in store may or may not include the things I've written, but I know they are better, even if they don't feel better or make sense, like quitting the job I prayed for. Our identities and our life's purpose are not based on our feelings, our families, a diagnosis, a job title, our pasts, or our circumstances. The Lord's plan will prevail. We were created to be a part of this story, His story.

He gave us the Bible that tells us who He is, who we are, and what our purpose is. It all points back to Jesus, and so should we. If all I do for the rest of my life is get to know the Lord more and more, I'm so okay with that. I don't want any accolades of this world, trophies, or titles. I just want Jesus. Jesus says to first love the Lord, then our neighbors as ourselves. We must prioritize love by receiving it and making it practical. To receive it, remember that humility precedes honor. There's not much to figure out, and in all your trying, it's not something you can earn, but still it's offered to you and available. If you feel like you can't figure it out, if you're tired of trying, or don't know who you really are or what your purpose is, I don't have the answers for you. Congrats, you read almost thirty thousand words for that, ha! But I can point you to who does have the answers. God does.

The opposite of hustle is peace, and that caught me off guard when I googled that. I seriously reloaded my browser and did a double take. God is peace. The opposite of hustle is peace. Isaiah 48:18 reads, *"Oh, that you had listened to my commands! Then you would have had peace flowing like a gentle river and righteousness rolling like the waves."* Lysa TerKeurst wrote about this peace, God's peace, better than I could have, in her book *What Happens When Women Say Yes to God and Walk in Faith.* She wrote that *"God chose such an interesting word to describe His peace—a river! A river is not calm and void of activity. It is active and cleansing and confident of the direction it is headed in. It doesn't get caught up with the rocks in its path. It flows over and around them, all the while smoothing their jagged edges and allowing them to add to its beauty rather than take away from it."* She wrote that *"the world's way to peace would have me pull back to make life a little easier for me, my circumstances, and my family. The problem with this is that we were not put here to be all about ourselves—we were put here to be all about God."* Leave the hustle and step into peace. Stop priding yourself in the hustle, like I did. Humility precedes honor. What if instead of hustling, you could be healing? When I was humbled enough in my search of self to realize I am not the main character, I learned more about He who is the main character, and my identity was redeemed. You are invited into this story by the main character. He is waiting for you.

2 Peter 3:9 says, *"The Lord isn't really being slow about his promise to return as some people think. No, he is being patient for your sake. He does not want anyone to perish, so he is giving more time for everyone to repent."*

What do you have to let go of? He is proposing to you, and He's waiting for you.

ABOUT THE AUTHOR

Danielle DeGarmo wrote "Identity Redemption," her first published book at 19 years old while living in Oklahoma City, OK, wearing mostly sweatpants and drinking cappuccinos. To connect with Danielle, or "Dani," as many call her, please email daniellefaith03@yahoo.com. She'd love to share a cappuccino, in person, or in spirit, with you!

Printed in the USA
CPSIA information can be obtained
at www.ICGtesting.com
LVHW091541111024
793460LV00002BA/323